When Your Long-Term Marriage Ends

A Workbook for Divorced Women

Elaine Newell

Resource Publications, Inc.
San Jose, California

Editorial director: Kenneth Guentert
Managing editor: Elizabeth J. Asborno
Copyeditor: Mary Ezzell

Reprint Department
Resource Publications, Inc.
160 E. Virginia Street #290
San Jose, CA 95112-5876

Library of Congress Cataloging in Publication Data
Newell, Elaine, 1931–
    When your long-term marriage ends : a workbook for divorced women /
    Elaine Newell.
            p.   cm.
    Includes bibliographical references.
    ISBN 0-89390-291-8
    1. Divorced women—Life skills guides. I. Title.
HQ814.N48   1994
306.89—dc20   94-405

Printed in the United States of America

98 97 96 95 94 | 5 4 3 2 1

Grateful acknowledgment is extended for permission to reprint the following:

Quotation from *A Course in Miracles* © 1975 Foundation for Inner Peace. Used by permission.

Front cover photo (background) taken by Perry Chow.
Front cover photo (left) taken by Pagar Studios (Milton Lower Falls, MA).
Front cover photo (right) taken by Elaine Newell.
Back cover photo taken by Morin's Studio, Milford, MA 01757.

To all those dear souls who
have helped me on my journey
to love and understanding

My teachers
Laurie and Carol

My parents
Orville and Winifred

My brother
Doc

My children
Peggy, Leslye, Michael, Eric

My husband
Jean Andre

And All the Countless Others

Thank you.

Contents

Preface

This book is written for the woman whose long-term marriage has ended—or is ending—in divorce. While the demise of any relationship is painful, the ending of a lifetime relationship carries unique emotional problems. To a large extent, this work is based on personal experience as well as interviews with numerous women; therefore, feminine pronouns are used throughout. There are differences between the sexes (happily!), and it is obvious that divorce is an Equal Opportunity Tester. It is also true that healing of the spirit is available to all who seek it. For this reason male readers are invited to glean from these pages whatever benefit they may find.

Blank pages have been included at the end of each chapter for your written notes and/or further responses to the exercises. You are encouraged to use them.

Introduction

A divorce certificate, like a marriage certificate, is a piece of paper. In reality neither makes the union or dissolves it. People do that. It is indeed rare for someone to walk out of a divorce court feeling emotionally free of a former spouse. That doesn't happen in a court room. It happens to different people in different places and different spaces, but when the decision to end the marriage has been made, this is ultimately what you are aiming for—Emotional Freedom, the final letting go of the marriage, of the past, and accepting with expectation your role as a single person. It also means accepting the person you are *today* and the person you were once married to as the person he is *today*.

For thirty-one years I shared a marriage with a handsome, intelligent, sometimes loving, always intriguing man. During this period the love I felt was total and unwavering. I would have, quite literally, jumped between him and the speeding bullet. Today I would duck. This does not mean the love is gone. It means it has changed. It means I have changed. And it means he has changed. *Change!* What a fearful word! And what a stumbling block to our growth process when we resist it.

After a divorce, in many ways you have been born again. You are facing a new phase of life, a new beginning, and quite like the babe who has just emerged from the womb, find everything new, strange. And like the babe, you will

1

pass through many stages of growth and development—some painful, some wondrous—but as you pass each milestone you become stronger, growing in self-confidence and self-esteem. In simplest terms, what you are left with when your marriage ends is your own life, your own future. In some cases that's the only thing you are left with. However, when you think about it, that's all you had when you came in—and really, that's quite a lot.

It is an important moment in your life when you discover for yourself the great Truth that things may happen around you, and things may happen to you, but the only things that really count are the things that happen in you.

— Eric Butterworth

Chapter 1

Accepting Responsibility

With the possible exception of tragedies that befall our children, there are few personal trials as gut-deep wounding as divorce. It slices and dices the ego as few experiences can. This is particularly true when infidelity is involved, which is the major cause of the demise of long-term marriages. This statement is in no way intended to diminish the pain one suffers at the death of a loved one, yet somehow death is eventually accepted as being the natural course of events. Divorce, on the other hand, is not natural. In spite of what statistics say (and they say a lot!), it is rare when a couple enters into marriage expecting to divorce.

As we ring down the curtain on the twentieth century, bolstered by slogans, mottos and paperback book titles entreating us to "Get Ours," "Have an Open Marriage," "Achieve Multiple Orgasms," ad infinitum, it is apparent to many that something is out of sync. In spite of what the tabloids tell us, we still hunger for togetherness, still yearn for a mate who will walk steadfast at our side down life's pot-holed highways. There is a need within the human spirit to share, be it a sunrise, a secret, an embrace, or a TV

3

show. The need to mate, not only in a sexual sense, is inherent in us.

Whether we are the petitioner of the divorce or the recipient, the aftermath of the event invariably opens a Pandora's box of unexplainable, unexpected, seemingly unresolvable emotional and physical complaints: sleeplessness, paralyzing depressions, anxiety attacks, rage, an inability to swallow, constipation, fear (sometimes bordering on terror), loneliness, sexual frustration—the list is a lengthy one. "Will I ever feel normal again?" is a common cry.

The answer is, "Yes, but...." We all need our comfort zone. We all feel violated when it is removed. But, "normal" is likely to be something quite different in our tomorrows than it was in our yesterdays. That doesn't mean it will be any the less comfortable or satisfying.

But let's be explicit here. What we are really looking for is peace—freedom from anger, resentment, jealousy and guilt; a place of contentment within ourselves. The good news is: This *is* possible to find, and there are logical steps we can take in order to do so. The not-so-good news is: It's hard work. While none of these steps are easy, and they do take time, they all lead upward, or rather inward, to where our only real peace resides.

It is natural for anyone in pain to want an instant fix. Unfortunately, many women (and men), in a desperate attempt to make the pain go away, unwittingly strike out on a path which exacerbates their turmoil. There is no instant fix for divorce. There is no pill, no shot, no drug no matter how potent, that is going to patch up our lives. But consider too the fact that there is no pain, physical, mental or emotional, which was not first the product of our own minds. Nor was there ever any joy, humor, or love that did not spring from the same source. It is necessary, therefore, to become aware of what is happening within our minds, for that is where our peace *and* our pain reside.

For a moment, for several moments, try stepping back and taking a look at your mind, as if you were an observer. Are your thoughts a chaotic jumble filled with imagined scenes of your spouse making love to someone else? Or a jagged-edged repartee of what you wish you'd said when

4

he said such-and-such? Do these scenes play over and over like a stuck record? Maybe you find yourself reliving again and again some painful real-life scene from the past. If this is so (and more often than not it is) you are suffering from The Victim Mentality. These tormenting images are banging away at your brain because you are seeing yourself as a victim. Putting an end to the chaos requires a change of thinking, an emptying of the thoughts that are causing you pain, and a refilling with the peace you want to be there. It is necessary to reprogram the mind, because peace cannot live in a mind at war against itself.

But how do we create this peace within? What is the magic key to finding what we so desperately desire? Peace of mind is achieved through an understanding of self—and an acceptance of self. At some level of consciousness we know when we are kidding ourselves, lying to ourselves, making excuses to ourselves for behavior or attitudes which fall short of our own ideal. This practice seeds the war within. If you would have a peaceful spirit, you must be honest with your self. Totally. You must be forgiving of self. Totally. And you must be accepting of your self as the totally unique human being you truly are.

Step One: Choose Where You Want to Go

The first step in your quest for peace is to remove yourself from the turbulent present and take a long hard look into the future. Where do you want to go? What kind of future do you want to have? We're not talking here about "What shall I do with the rest of my life?" but rather some really serious thinking about what kind of a person you want to be after the dust has settled. And make no mistake about it—you will be changed. You'll be okay—if that's what you choose—but you will be changed.

You are who you are today because of who you were yesterday, because of what you *thought* yesterday. Today you are building the structure of your future through your thoughts, attitudes and ideas. You are at a point in your life now where choices must be made; don't kid yourself, drifting with the tide and refusing to make decisions are also choices, and probably not ones you will be too happy with later on. What you decide now will have a lot to say about your future, so spend as much time as is necessary in determining what kind of woman you want to be in your tomorrow. Think of the divorced women you know. Are they the kind of people you want to emulate? How has their divorce experience shaped their lives? Listed below are a few people whom you probably already know. They are who they are because of the choices they have made.

- The woman who adopted the role of the "swinging single" and patched up her wounded ego with a series of affairs, booze or other drugs.

- The woman who gave in to bitterness. She hasn't said a kind word about any man since her husband left her for another woman fifteen years ago.

- The woman who sought revenge by turning her children and friends against her former husband.

- The woman who has tied herself inexorably to the past with bonds of hate. Like Robert Burns' *Good Wife Kate*, she spends a lot of time around her hearth, nursing her wrath to keep it warm.

- The woman who used the children, money, or other forms of emotional blackmail to get whatever she felt she deserved from her former mate.

- The woman who simply grew cold and withdrew from life.

- The woman who has accepted what occurred and sees it as the best for both her and her former mate. She has established new relationships and a new life.

- The woman who maintains a friendship with her former husband, but has freed herself emotionally in order to pursue new relationships.

Naturally there are many other choices, but you get the idea. Of the eight possibilities outlined above, only two are positive. Human nature being what it is, we all tend to take the easy way out, especially when we are under stress. It's easier to blame than to accept our share of responsibility. It's easier to be angry rather than compassionate. It's easier to be judgmental instead of forgiving.

As you contemplate this first step of deciding where you want to go, it is important to be gentle with yourself. As you set your ideal, your goals, and begin working toward them, remember that humans react to trauma in human ways. Know that anger, bitterness, jealousy and guilt are but phases, stages you pass through on your way to tomorrow. Since these stages are undeniably uncomfortable, why should you want to stop here? Why should you want to get mired down in negative emotions when positive ones feel so much better? The sooner you begin to move out of the chaos and onto the next phase, the sooner you will begin to feel better.

Step Two: Accept Responsibility for Your Self

While Step One looks to the future, Step Two looks at the past. Accepting your share of responsibility for where you are is not easy. It requires objectivity and a fair amount of challenging of self. But why is this necessary, you ask? After all, he was the one who.... If it hadn't been for his.... The truth is he was a participant in the relationship, the same way you were a participant. He has his own share of responsibility. What we are looking at now is *you*.

Acknowledging your feelings, no matter what they may be, is a requirement for finding peace within. Denial is part of our human nature. We don't want to see what we don't want to see. Self-examination, getting in touch with our feelings, is a crucial step toward healing. Maybe there's anger there. Why should it be otherwise? Of course you're angry. Your world is collapsing. Acknowledge that anger. It's all right to be human. Later in this book there is an entire chapter devoted to anger and constructive ways of dealing with it, but for now, simply acknowledging that it is there is all that's required.

What about fear? Jealousy? Love? Hate? Resentment? Sadness? Disappointment? If you are honest with yourself, you will find all of these emotions and many, many more. All of us who have experienced divorce have experienced these same emotions. I assure you they will pass, with time. How much time is entirely up to you. It depends on your attitude—your willingness and eagerness to heal.

Looking at negative emotions is painful. Looking at an uncharted future is frightening, and accepting responsibility for both can be overwhelming. This is nothing that needs to be done in a frenzy. You don't have to steamroll. Take time to allow yourself to feel fully every emotion that surfaces. Admit that the emotion is there, that it is real. Pamper yourself, and always, always *take your time.*

Here is an exercise I encourage you to utilize each and every day, no matter how full—or empty—your days may be. Find a time each day when you can be completely alone.

> Find a quiet time, a quiet place where you know
> you will not be disturbed, maybe a warm,
> relaxing tub.
>
> Pour in some bubble bath...Swish it around...
> Make plenty of bubbles.
>
> Turn off the phone and put your favorite music
> on the cassette player. You don't want it loud...
> just a soft, gentle background...a setting.
>
> Now slip into the water...slowly...gently...
> allowing your body to experience the soothing
> peace of the water.

This is your private oasis...a place of private peace...and one *you* have created. You have taken the responsibility to do this for yourself.

That's right...relax...let go of the burdens...the cares...the troubling thoughts....Clear your mind as nearly as possible and when you are ready... let's quietly....gently...think about...EGO... *Ego...ego....*

Oh, you know her...She's that persona we show to the world...that protective shield we cloak ourself in. We sometimes get her confused with Self-Esteem, but she's very different. Ego is to the body what Self-Esteem is to the spirit.

Now, let's bring Ego out here...talk to her...take a good look at her...then calmly, but firmly, allow yourself to put her aside...for a while...

That's right! Hide her there beneath the soap bubbles. Just let her slip away and rest for a few minutes while you get in touch with Self-Esteem...the real you...your Higher Self...your Inner Voice. You may call this real part of you by a variety of names...God, Spirit, Energy, Conscience...whatever...the name doesn't matter. We all have it and we all know we have it.

Now look within these depths, within your center, and gently ask yourself if there is even the slightest possibility that you may, in some way, be responsible for being where you are today. Don't concentrate on the breakup of the marriage; go past that...go *deeper* than that. Have your thoughts, actions, reactions, in any way contributed to the person you are today? Are the patterns you learned in childhood still being used unconsciously just because they are familiar? Are these patterns something you would like to change? Are your attitudes, feelings and thoughts what you would like them to be?

9

Forget blame...Forget about feeling sorry for yourself because of what your parents did or didn't do...what your spouse did or didn't do. Ego is asleep now, remember? Guilt and blame are elements of her realm. You are somewhere else now. Remember what you thought, what you felt, what you did to shape your life. Look at the past with as little emotion as possible. Be very, very gentle with yourself, for you are a very special, wonderful and unique person. Just be objective. We are all human. We all make mistakes and we all have victories, times of nobility and times of defeat.

You will realize now, at a deep level, that you share something...*everything*, with everyone else. You are human. And you are spirit as well...just like everyone else.

Now...before you let go of this moment of communion, take an instant more to congratulate yourself on your accomplishment. You have just taken the first, firm step toward accepting responsibility for yourself, the mind/spirit self. The self entrusted to you by your Creator. And you will allow yourself this time of communion tomorrow, and tomorrow, and tomorrow, and for all your tomorrows. You will have this time of peace and introspection, this time of learning about this unique person called "you," because you deserve it.

Okay, it's time to let *ego...Ego...EGO*...back in from under the soap bubbles. Here she comes! Up and running again! Banging her drum as she marches through your mind...through your life.

But maybe...just maybe...she's a little panicked now that you were able...and willing...to put her aside for a moment. That's all right. She'll get used to it...in time.

Exercises

As much as possible, remove yourself emotionally from what is going on, and make a sustained effort (during the first part of this exercise) to answer these questions from an intellectual point of view rather than an emotional one. It won't be easy, but do your best.

1. Name three things that have happened to you that you sincerely feel are someone else's fault.

2. Name three areas where *you* have taken responsibility for your life. (These must be areas that are new—that have occurred since the divorce/separation.)

3. List the names of three women, preferably divorced, whom you admire.

4. List the character traits you admire in each of these women.

5. Do you want to be like these women? Would you want to change places with any of them? Would you want to make any of the traits you see in them part of your own life? Explain.

6. For the remainder of these exercises, move back into your emotional self. Feel the pain, anger, jealousy, frustration, disappointment—whatever it is you are having trouble with, whatever it is that is prohibiting you from moving out of this place—and write it down. Be deeply honest. No one but you is going to see what you have written unless you so choose. Now take a look, a *real* look at what is going on inside. Take all the time and paper you need. (Use the "Notes and Reflections" page, if you like.)

7. What would you like to change about what you wrote in response to number 6? You don't have to know how; you just have to know what.

8. List three things you can do, right now or when you get home, that will make you feel better.

9. When was the last time you did these "bettering" things for yourself? *Be honest!*

10. Spend the next few minutes communicating with your Higher Power, God, whatever you call the Universal Force. Tell your Higher Power how you really feel. Ask for your Higher Power's help. (You may write it down, if you like.)

Notes and Reflections

The process of spiritual growth is a difficult one because it is conducted against a natural resistance to keep things the way they were, to cling to the old map and the old ways, to take the easy path.

— M. Scott Peck

Chapter 2

Getting Help

S ome seemingly stoic individuals march through life with stiff upper lip and head held high, never venturing an outstretched hand for help or comfort, never admitting, even to themselves, that they need help in any form. Occasionally we hear these people referred to as "strong," but a closer look tells a different story. These troubled hearts are often filled with fear—fear that they have lost control of their lives, fear that there is no one, nothing "out there" that can help them, fear that others will see their hopelessness. Reaching out for help is an act of courage, an indication that we have the inner strength and awareness to know we do not have solutions to life's problems neatly catalogued in a leatherbound book.

Chances are good that you are not one of those who refuses to help herself; otherwise you would not be reading this book. But just in case there are little doubts creeping into your mind about the advisability of going for help, I strongly suggest you stamp out these negative thoughts the moment they enter. We all need help at some point. Needing help is one of life's experiences, and it comes to us all whether we live in a cave or a palace. There is truth in the old maxim, "No man is an island."

However, acknowledging our need for help is only a first step; we must follow through and seek out help, since it seldom comes knocking at our doors. That may sound glib, but it is amazing how emotionally paralyzed we can become when facing unfamiliar waters. We fear making a mistake, doing the wrong thing. Rest assured, reaching out for help is not a mistake, it is a step in the right direction. Procrastination is a deadly enemy.

In times of crisis (such as divorce!), buried garbage tends to surface. If your childhood was something less than a positive experience due to neglect, abuse, or any of a hundred other negativities, the likelihood that you'll be revisiting those problems now is strong. Your defenses are down, and that's when all the "stuff" you've buried gains strength. It is best to deal with it as it surfaces, and there is a very good reason for this. Dealing with your past will inevitably put you in touch with your present—maybe not only with the reasons for the divorce, but with the reasons for the marriage as well. Let's not overlook the most common fallout of divorce: depression. It's a rare bird indeed who can go through this period without, at some point, being deeply depressed. This is part of the experience of divorce, and one that will pass, if you allow it to pass. A very wise woman once said, "The only way to get better is to not like feeling worse."

Where then is the best place to look for help, and in what form? This depends on your particular circumstances. If alcohol is or ever was a problem in your life, attend AA, Al-Anon, or Adult Children of Alcoholics meetings—as often as possible. If child abuse or incest is part of your history, seek out the appropriate support group. Today (thankfully!) there are Twelve-Step Programs available for just about any trauma. Incidentally, these programs are thus called because of their basic structure, which originated with Alcoholics Anonymous. There are of course support programs which are not patterned after the Twelve Steps, but only after personal investigation can you draw your own conclusion as to whether or not a certain program is right for you.

If you have a minister who is an informed professional counselor, enlist his/her help. If he/she isn't a trained counselor, it is best to look elsewhere. Seeing no counselor is better than seeing a poor counselor. I would also avoid counseling with your minister if he/she is on close terms with your ex-husband. The days of mediation are over. You've gotten (or are getting) a divorce. A professional therapist, preferably one who specializes in family/divorce problems, is your best and safest bet, but please check him/her out. Incidentally, a female therapist will probably be of more benefit to a female client, not because of bias but because of innate understanding. Ask for referrals from your friends who have been through similar situations. If you're living in a new city, look up names in the Yellow Pages under Social Workers or Family Counseling. Ask questions over the phone about credentials, years of experience, and specialty areas; when you go in for an appointment, ask pertinent questions regarding personal views about marriage and male/female relationships before agreeing to become a client. You can pretty well tell if you are on the same wavelength after a thirty-minute interview. If the counselor is antagonistic, or expresses ideas foreign to your gut feelings, look further. Part of accepting responsibility for yourself is learning to trust yourself. Learn to listen to your intuition, to your Inner Voice.

An adjunct to private counseling is becoming increasingly popular—divorce therapy groups. These groups work exceedingly well for some people; for others, not at all. Some people begin with private counseling and later move on to group therapy. Both are valuable. It's a matter of personal choice.

There is another resource that is open to you without charge, but before using it, I caution you to be highly selective in this area as well. That resource is family and friends. The simple fact that these people care about you instills them with a certain amount of prejudice. They want to help you, and they very probably think your former mate is a real jerk, or worse, and may not hesitate to say so. The problem here is that when someone begins maligning someone we loved—or still love—we feel a need to jump to his defense. What often happens is that this type of "bad mouthing" tends to strengthen our tie to our ex-mate rather than loosen it. What you do need from your family and friends is a listening post, someone who will sit and listen to you pour it all out, without condemnation of you or your former spouse.

In my own case, my family and some of my friends, although tremendously supportive, were not aware of my need to talk it out. Whenever I brought up the subject they changed it. They did not see that this was my way of mourning. I made it a point to enlarge my circle of friends by finding new ones who would listen to whatever I needed to say. Actually this was a twofold benefit because most of my new friends were divorced and knew what I was going through.

Very often, people with whom you work and who do not know your former mate are the best listening posts, and sometimes they can offer the least prejudiced advice—if you're in the market for hearing it, that is!

However, since you are accepting responsibility for your life, since you are building your future, it is necessary to weigh any and all advice you receive against your personal criteria. If you act on the advice given, will it take you where you want to go? I am personally convinced that unless your friend has been through a divorce she cannot, no matter how well meaning, truly put herself in your shoes. It's pretty much akin to a male doctor explaining to a first-time mother how labor contractions are going to feel. He might have all the theory in the world, but if you don't have the pain you just simply don't know what it feels like. When it comes to advice, consider it carefully. Then take the best and leave the rest.

We have talked about reprograming—dumping from your mind what is not wanted and filling it with what is. Self-help reading material and some good cassette tapes are ideal tools for your reprograming. Choose titles that address your particular need. A few highly accredited psychologists have some excellent self-help tapes on the market. Play these on your car cassette player while driving to work. Play them while you lounge in your bubble bath or while you're getting dressed in the morning. Play them at night while you're falling asleep. Repetition is extremely important. Most of us do not accept information the first time we hear it; but if the message is something you want to believe, and you know it is good helpful advice, then you can make it a part of your mind by programing it into your subconscious. Your conscious mind may be giving you fits right now, but it is at the subconscious level where damage or aid really happens. Be good to yourself. Put in what you know you need and eventually it will become a part of your conscious thinking. Subliminal tapes can also be of value, especially while you're falling asleep, but logical, intelligent messages that make sense to *you*, in language that makes sense to *you*, are your best bet.

There are many "New Age" groups that can be helpful in putting you in touch with the "inner you." A few of these groups are pretty far out, but others—the better ones—will gently, subtly, open doors to new and enlightened ways of thinking. We're talking now of spiritual enlightenment, which has absolutely nothing to do with organized religion. "Spiritual enlightenment" is another way of saying "awareness of your Creator, God, Energy, Higher Self, Conscience," or whatever you've chosen to call your inner voice.

Another benefit of "New Age" is its emphasis on meditation. The reason is pretty obvious; through meditation we get in touch with our Inner Voice. There are other ways to do this, such as hypnosis or daydreaming, but in meditation we learn to listen to what is going on inside. If meditation is a new experience for you, don't be put off by the so-called mysteries of it. Meditation is no more mysterious than prayer. In prayer we talk to our Creator. In meditation we listen to what He/She has to say. The benefits of meditation, however brief (a three-minute session will do to start), cannot be overrated. Meditation is excellent for inducing relaxation; it can clear the mind of cacophony and it can reenergize as well. It is worth the time and effort it may take to learn.

There are numerous books on the market that espouse various techniques. Most are unnecessarily complicated. The simplest and most effective way to learn meditation is with a candle. Try the following:

Find a quiet, relatively dark place where you will not be disturbed. Place the candle a comfortable distance away from you— eighteen to twenty-four inches is good. Light the candle and stare at the flame while you take several really deep breaths. Concentrate on the candle. After five or six breaths, allow your eyes to close slowly. Then try to visualize the candle flame in your mind's eye. Think only of the flame. If you've stared at it intently enough you will very quickly see its image displayed on your inner screen. When it begins to fade, gently pull it back into view with your mind (still with your eyes closed). After a couple of minutes or so open your eyes.

That's it! You have just taken a first step in focusing your mind. With practice your technique will improve. The idea here is to focus your mind on one thing and one thing only. Later, you may concentrate on an affirmation, for example, "I am at peace" or "I am relaxed" or "I am strong and filled with energy"—whatever feels right for you. One of the benefits of meditation is an ever-increasing degree of tranquility. If you practice daily you will begin to experience the benefits within a relatively short period of time. A word of caution: Don't get disturbed if you feel you're not "getting anywhere" in your meditations. This is a common complaint. The benefits are often subtle and always highly individualized. There is no right or wrong way to do it.

During the research for this book, I found, to my surprise, that my reactions to my divorce experience were not as unique as I thought. The more women I talked with, the more I realized that their experiences mirrored my own. Some of this can be attributed to generational influences, the patterning and value systems instilled in us in our youth. For me, youth was "The Golden Age of Movies." My formative years were influenced strongly by Hollywood films, heroes and heroines. Men and women had wills of steel and hearts of gold. No matter how far a man strayed from the straight and narrow, he was still a good guy at heart and always regained his senses before the last reel ended. Naturally the heroine sacrificed all for love, home and family. These heroines were my idols. These were the people and life situations I unconsciously emulated. I found that I shared these fantasies with thousands of others.

Once on the path to spiritual growth and emotional freedom, I came to realize that I had, in a very real sense, been worshipping at the wrong altar. My marriage, my husband, my home, my family were my god. In time my awareness reached the point where I realized that no matter how much I love these people and possessions, they are all exterior to me. My real God (which is what I choose to call my Inner Voice) is an interior force. It is not only a part of me—it is me. The letting go of the false belief that other people carry the key to my happiness and my identity was a slow and painful process, but one that was very necessary if I was to achieve my goal of becoming the woman I wanted to be.

If you are a woman who, like so many others, has denied your selfhood in favor of those you love—in essence put your own interests on the back burner—the chance that you will benefit from some "New Age" concepts is highly likely.

One concept which has been attributed to "New Age" is the use of affirmations, but this is actually an ancient practice and common throughout the Bible, most obviously in the Book of Psalms. Let's look for a moment at what affirmations are and why they work.

An affirmation is in essence a positive thought. The reason affirmations work (and the reason why their counterpart, negative statements, work too) is because, as we have previously stated, everything begins in the mind: love and hate, health and sickness, strength and weakness, joy and sorrow, abundance and need—absolutely all. The process is so simple it often goes unnoticed. For example, if you tell yourself you aren't feeling well, and you reinforce that a couple of times, soon your body picks up the message and reacts accordingly. On the other hand when you affirm your physical well being and reinforce that thought a few times, you will very shortly experience good health. However, the body is not easily fooled, so it will not respond according to such input unless it totally believes the message it has received; that total belief begins in the mind. In other words, just saying you feel a certain way isn't enough.

Your mind has to believe what you are saying to your body. Any medical doctor can tell you how extraordinarily effective the hypochondriac's negative messages are. He literally makes himself sick. The same doctor will also tell you that the patients who have positive attitudes are the ones who heal. The reason for this is that the mind accepts whatever you "program" it to accept (which is why we've talked so much about reprograming!). If you would be in control of your life, you must first be in control of your mind. The mind accepts what is continually fed to it and manifests this information into physical form. It is important to remember that a lighthearted, occasional affirmation will be lost if counteracted by a slew of negative thoughts. Affirmations only work if they are continually reinforced.

Let's take the example of weight loss. If you notice your clothes getting a little tight and decide you want to lose a few pounds, try this little experiment. Begin by looking at yourself in the mirror each morning, noon and night and saying to that image, "I am slim. I am beautiful. My body is the ideal weight. I now weigh x pounds." *Be explicit, be firm, and above all believe what you are saying*. If you do this you will, very soon, begin to lose weight *if* you do not counteract your positive thoughts with continual thoughts of chocolate cake, gooey desserts, and "Oh, I'm too fat." Each time these counterproductive thoughts come to mind, instantly replace them with your affirmation. No one ever ate anything without thinking about eating it first. Practice this consistently for a month and you will throw away your diet book forever because affirmations work. (Please note! I am not talking here about obesity. Although affirmations will help, real food addiction, as with any addiction, requires professional therapy.)

This brings us back to our old theme, "You are what you think." Decide what it is you want to be and affirm it. Write it down, stick it on your mirror, carry it in your purse, pin it to your pillow, and it will become your reality.

A word of caution: Affirmations are for yourself because you are the only person you can control. Affirmations do not work if we try to use them to control others. "John is going to fall in love with me" is not an affirmation. "I am loved; I am lovable" is.

One other point should be stressed before leaving the subject of this collective thing called the New Age. Real New Age ideas are about as far removed from the "Me Generation" of the '60s as heaven is from hell. While the thrust of the '60s was initially toward self-awareness, it quickly became misdirected toward an attitude of rebellion and selfishness. If enough people agree on convoluting anything, it will certainly happen, but it is important to keep in mind that true spiritual concepts express the belief that all are equal, each is important, and wholeness/oneness with our Creator is the one goal.

Up to now we've been talking about ways and means of working your way through your period of crisis by confronting your problems. While this is vital, it is also important to occasionally "take a break." There are other groups and organizations that will not only be an aid in your growth toward emotional freedom but will likely offer a certain degree of peace of mind along the way. These groups will be highly individualized and should be chosen to suit your own particular interests. The reasoning behind getting involved in other activities is, in a word, respite. When we are under stress we need to get away from our problems for brief periods of time. The way to do this is to become involved in something you are truly interested in, something that has absolutely nothing to do with your divorce, ex-mate, or anything related to that situation.

For example, if you have a knack for amateur theatricals, seek out your local Little Theater group. Nearly every small town or community has one. How you choose to participate is immaterial—whether before the footlights, painting scenery, helping out with props, or any one of a dozen different backstage jobs. Do whatever pleases you. If you've ever been involved in Little Theater, you know these activities require time and concentration. They also give you something else to think about, somewhere else to put your energies, and they offer a marvelous opportunity for team play. Besides, most of the people engaged in Little Theater are fun, upbeat, and interesting—precisely the type of company you need.

If you respond to this suggestion with, "Oh, I could never do anything like that" or "I just don't have the time or energy," realize this is a copout. If you are being honest with yourself (a requirement for healing), then face the fact that if you are dragging your feet about doing something different, new, or exciting, you are, at some level, enjoying being stuck in your rut and wallowing in your pain. Which is okay—for a while. Just don't make it your life's occupation. When you are ready, and the sooner the better, get out and do something. Being a couch potato should not be an option now.

Amateur theatricals are not your thing? Then how about an art course, a study group, aerobics, yoga, ceramics classes, a travel club, joining a chorus, or helping out with a political campaign? Whatever interests you! And if you've lost interest in everything, a common symptom of the depression which accompanies divorce, then turn back the pages of time and remember what it was that used to interest you. Then go out and join up. This step takes a considerable amount of self-discipline, but if you keep in mind your goal of becoming that person you want to be, it will be easier to make that first phone call, that first contact. You have more to gain from exposure to outside activities than just shared interests. There is the opportunity to meet new people, open yourself up to new experiences, and stop that #%$*&#@* record from spinning around in your head. In short, getting involved and interested in other people and activities is an important step in your reprograming.

Another must is exercise. Fifteen minutes each day will produce benefits in a number of ways. It releases tension, it helps trim the body, and it improves physical health. The greatest benefit, however, is that it teaches self-discipline. Anybody can find fifteen minutes somewhere in their day, and disciplining yourself to do so is another way of gaining control of your life.

Now let's do a quick review of the required steps to healing:

1. Treat yourself to a minimum of fifteen minutes of solitude each day, preferably in a bubble bath.

2. Work out the "garbage" by joining a support group, e.g. a Twelve-Step Program that addresses a problem area or issue in your past.

3. Seek out a professional therapist who is skilled in divorce issues, one who will help you to identify your feelings and get in touch with them. This may include a divorce therapy group.

4. Talk out your feelings with family, friends, or coworkers. "Dump" on people who will listen to you objectively.

5. Reprogram your mind with positive input through the use of cassette tapes and reading material.

6. Use affirmations—continually.

7. Deepen your spiritual awareness by joining groups who can help you get in touch with your Higher Self, God Self, Inner Voice, or whatever you choose to call your spiritual nature.

8. Learn to meditate. This practice will help you relax, help you sleep, and help increase your energy level.

9. Get involved in some outside fun activity.

10. Get a minimum of fifteen minutes of vigorous exercise every day.

If you practice these with even a moderate amount of dedication, you will heal from your divorce; you will regain your emotional freedom. The time it takes varies, but you can be assured that within a few weeks you will begin to notice improvement.

Practice eight of these ten steps and you have an eighty percent chance of regaining your emotional health and emotional freedom.

Practice five steps and you cut your chance in half.

The decision is yours.

Exercises

Indicate with a "T" or an "F" whether the following statements are True or False. There are no right or wrong responses. Honesty is the key that unlocks the dam of pent-up or unrecognized emotions. Be as honest with yourself as you can be.

_____ I consider myself a courageous person.

_____ I consider myself a troubled person.

_____ I see my current state of affairs as life changing.

_____ I see my current emotional problems as temporary.

_____ In ten words or less I can define my problems.

_____ I know of a self-help program that deals with my current situation.

_____ If I am not moving forward at the end of six weeks, I will consider private counseling.

1. If your response to the last statement was "True," explain what you think private counseling with a professional mental health therapist would do for you.

2. I feel more comfortable with men/women.

☐ Yes

☐ No

Explain:

3. I only talk with (or unload on) people who I think will be sympathetic to my point of view.

☐ Yes

☐ No

4. I am unwilling to listen to an objective point of view from someone I can trust.

☐ Yes

☐ No

5. I am willing to set aside at least one hour a day for healing.

☐ Yes

☐ No

6. I am willing to consciously feel emotional pain in order to work it through, cleanse myself, and let the pain go.

☐ Yes

☐ No

7. I am willing to try meditation to calm my mind and help me find some inner peace.

☐ Yes

☐ No

8. If I choose to try meditation, I will make a commitment to do this for a five-minute period, once each day, for one week.

☐ Yes

☐ No

9. If I choose exercise as a means of helping me feel better, I will make a commitment of fifteen minutes a day, for three weeks.

☐ Yes

☐ No

10. If I choose affirmations as a means of helping me feel better, I will make a commitment to write down a new affirmation each day and repeat it at least five times throughout that day, for a period of three weeks.

☐ Yes

☐ No

11. Although "happiness" and "fun" are not part of my present vocabulary, I will make a promise to myself to seek out something that might be fun, at least once a week. (Preferably, this will be an activity that involves other people).

☐ Yes

☐ No

After reading the next question, spend a minimun of three minutes really thinking about it before answering. It's amazing how many of us say and think we want one thing, when we really want another.

12. Remembering that the only thing I have left of my marriage is the pain I carry in my heart, and admitting that when I let that pain go I will have nothing left of my marriage, I am willing to let that pain go and face the void.

☐ Yes

☐ No

Notes and Reflections

Notes and Reflections

Heaven has no rage like love to hatred turned,
Nor hell a fury like a woman scorned.

— William Congreve

Chapter 3

Dealing with Anger

I t's okay to get angry when someone rocks our boat. And it's okay to get very angry when someone sinks it.

One journey has ended and you are now beginning a new one. This time you are not only captain of the ship, you are also the map-maker. You are charting the course. It is a new adventure, one to be filled with new dreams and new goals, but before grabbing hold of the new it is necessary to come to terms with the demise of the first. Part of that transition includes working through the anger— and letting it go.

Anger is always a destructive force for the one who holds it, and the one who holds it is the one most damaged by the anger. However, anger is a human emotion and not one to be denied.

In the aftermath of divorce your anger may erupt in one wingding of an outburst, or it may come in a series of outbursts. It may take the form of bawling your eyes out and pounding your pillow, or it may be a slow-burning fire whose embers continually lie waiting to be fanned into a blaze. Often it manifests as illness—hypertension, heart trouble, ulcers, mental disease, cancer, or any number of other ailments.

Guilt is another form of anger, and just as illness is anger taken out on our bodies, guilt too is directed at ourselves. Few of us have led such exemplary lives that we have no regrets for past behavior, but it is important to recognize the difference between guilt and regret. The former is a heavy, self-punishing load; the latter a healthy form of self-evaluation, which once examined is then gently laid aside.

Some of us are so frightened by anger in any form that we literally live our lives denying its existence within ourselves and go to great extremes to avoid it in others. Let's be real. Avoiding anger is as impossible as avoiding laughter. However, denying it is highly possible and unfortunately too often practiced. How then do we recognize this negative emotion and work through it?

1. Bring it out.

2. Deal with it.

3. Let it go.

This process is vital if we are to achieve mental health and emotional freedom.

It will be helpful for you to remind yourself from time to time that you are in a temporary period of vulnerability. If you should do something that in retrospect you feel was irrational or out of character for you, have the compassion to forgive yourself, especially if it is something you would forgive in others who were in the same set of circumstances.

Bring It Out

If you are the type of person who throws things—dishes, glasses, telephones—when you're heated up, chances are you've already made it through bringing it out—if, that is, you are facing the real reason for the anger. For example, if you blow up over being accidentally shortchanged at the supermarket, the real cause of your anger may be that your ex neglected to send this month's child-support check.

Being brutally honest with yourself about what is going on inside isn't always as easy as you may think. It requires constant monitoring.

If you are the type who holds anger inside and allows it to fester, the following suggestions are for you.

1. Acknowledge the truth that your feelings are of equal importance to the feelings of everyone else. Not more. Not less. *Equal.*

2. Try thinking about your divorce experience as though it had happened to someone else, someone you care about. If possible, make your own cassette recording of the story and play it back often. But remember, it is not your story, it belongs to someone else.

3. Now ask yourself, "Would I feel angry if my friend had been hurt in the way just described above?" If the answer is "yes," go back and read #1 again. If you answer "no," repeat #2. Repeat these steps as often as necessary until you can feel truly angry at what has happened to *you!* Many of us are able to empathize with someone else's pain, but our protective shield (ego) prohibits us from experiencing our own. Depending on your temperament, this first step of bringing out the anger may be accomplished quickly, or it may take a considerable amount of time. Do not bypass it, but be gentle with yourself and move at your own pace.

Deal with It

Dealing with the anger is what really frightened us about bringing it out. We knew that bringing out the anger meant we would have to deal with it. Once you get past the first step, however, you will probably find yourself almost eager to deal with it so you can reach the point where you can finally get release by letting it go. Not many people enjoy being angry, so working through it as quickly—and as thoroughly—as possible is immensely rewarding.

The following is a little vignette from my own experience, which I think will point out what is meant by bringing out the anger and dealing with it. For me, bringing it out was the tough part; once it surfaced, the dealing was easy—and instantaneous.

It took me a long time, several years in fact, to make the decision to divorce. It was a terribly difficult and emotionally charged period. However, once I set my course, I began keeping a tight rein on my emotions. I kept reminding myself that the marriage was over so there was no longer any reason to argue or wail. I foolishly thought I could turn off my emotions as easily as I could turn off a faucet. I was wrong.

The house had been sold, the division of worldly goods accomplished. My almost-ex was getting ready to move in with his girlfriend, and we were both making herculean efforts to be practical as well as polite. The only things remaining in our home now belonged to him and he was in the process of boxing them up. To his credit he had gone out of his way to help me get reestablished in my new apartment and had worked long and hard at hanging curtain rods and bookcases and doing all the "mechanical" things that were such a mystery to me. One Friday night when I returned to the apartment, I found him stretched out on the living room floor, obviously exhausted. I complimented him on how well everything had shaped up, and he suggested we go out to dinner "to celebrate" the completion of the task. Since I was tired too, the idea had appeal.

The dinner was pleasant, familiar, a little too comfortable. It was easy to forget, for a few moments, what was happening to our lives. We took our time, leisurely lingering over the meal, both apparently reluctant to let it go. Finally, there wasn't an excuse to stay longer and we headed back to my apartment. He was driving.

The car had scarcely pulled out of the parking lot when I sensed a feeling of tension in the air. My chauffeur gave a little cough and sort of redistributed his body weight, one of those unconscious signals that told me I wasn't going to like what was coming.

I didn't.

"You know," he said in a somewhat strained voice, "now that you're settled into the apartment I think, well, if you should for any reason, ummm, if you need to come back to the house for any reason, maybe you should call first."

"Oh? Why's that?" I asked cautiously.

"Well, ummm, _____ (name deleted to protect the guilty!) wants to come by to pick out what she wants to take to her place and what we'll be putting into storage."

There wasn't a weapon handy so I used what I had. I hit him over the head with my purse. He ducked, struggling to keep control of the wheel.

"You want to walk your #*&%$%* through the ruins of our marriage so she can pick over the spoils?" I landed another blow, furious I had only the small cloth purse instead of my usual saddlebag. "You want her to check out our possessions of thirty years to see if they're *good* enough for her?" I swung again. "If that, that *woman* comes *near* my home I'll run her over as she waddles up the driveway!" Another direct hit! By this time he had given up all attempt to view the road and was huddled against the driver's door, still gripping the steering wheel with one hand while trying to protect his head with the other.

"Okay! Okay!" he shrieked. "I'm sorry I mentioned it!"

"I'll bet you are!" I screamed and landed one final blow, then retreated to the passenger side of the car.

From the other seat I heard a long hissing sound. Something like, "Whweee." We finished the five-minute drive in icy silence.

I am not condoning physical violence. (Actually the pain inflicted on this occasion was much more emotional than physical.) Nor am I saying that my way of dealing with this situation (or one similar) is the only way. The point is that in a matter of a few explosive seconds I, number one, brought out the anger and two, dealt with it. There wasn't the slightest doubt in my mind (or his) about the reason for my anger. I was mad with a capital "P" at the insult and insensitivity of his remark. I was furious that some other woman was getting half my possessions and my husband, and I was enraged at losing my home. The hell with keeping a stiff upper lip! The hell with denying I was hurt and angry! The hell with trying to act civilized when I felt most assuredly uncivilized! When it was over I felt enormously better for having let the truth be known. I hadn't hidden it. I hadn't pretended something I did not feel. I had been one hundred percent honest. This was not the only occasion when I laid my cards on the table. There were numerous subsequent incidents when I expressed my deepest feelings and consequently eventually ridded myself of the negativity, although I don't recall another incident that was quite so explosive. I believe that the friendship I have today with my former husband is a direct result of that honesty.

Each of us has our own way; the key is to deal with the real issues and not hide from them.

As pointed out earlier, infidelity is a major factor in the breakup of long-term marriages and therefore needs to be addressed here. While many divorce decrees list adultery as the cause, I personally believe it is more likely the effect. Chemical dependency, uncontrolled compulsions, boredom, lack of commitment, mid-life crises, loss (or fear of loss) of sex drive, diminished self-esteem, loss of a job, an empty nest, and any number of other human problems are the real causes. Adultery is a sequential event whose roots are in the initial, underlying problem. If infidelity is not part of your history the following pages may still be of interest because we are looking at the nature of anger in general as well as how it applies to this particular issue.

There is an old proverb that says, "Before you can judge a man it is necessary to walk a mile in his shoes." I suggest that this is also true for The Other Woman. This is not a sympathetic excuse for husband stealing, but it is highly egotistical to expect others to live by our moral standards. There is something else to consider, too. No woman ever stole a husband without his full cooperation. However, if you have never been a single woman in love with a married man, it is difficult to understand the tumult of feelings this situation evokes within her: jealousy, envy, longing for something just out of reach.

Consider also, that there are women (and men) who due to psychological or emotional problems are attracted only to people who are unavailable. Undoubtedly this dysfunction carries with it a considerable amount of anguish.

Few titles conjure up such vivid images as the one we call The Other Woman. She is seductive, scheming, greedy, manipulative, completely without morals, young and always breathtakingly beautiful. She caters to a man's every need and of course knows all the tricks of the world's oldest profession. Wrong! Studies on the subject tell us that in the majority of cases men who have left their wives for greener pastures say, in retrospect, the sex was better at home than in the new relationship.

The women I interviewed offered the following description of The Other Woman. She is physically less attractive than the wife (usually outweighs her by twenty to one hundred pounds); she is from a lower socio/economic level, less educated, younger by ten to as much as twenty years; she has an abrasive, often domineering personality, is less nurturing, and possesses minimal domestic skills. Then what, pray tell, other than youth, was the attraction? There are as many answers to that as there are extra-marital affairs. It is safe to say, however, The Other Woman filled a need within these men that they perceived was not being fulfilled by their wives. This is not to say the need was always positive; some people have a psychological need for pain. In the cases involving chemical dependency, the need is undoubtedly an unconscious desire to suffer—to be punished, even humiliated—coupled with a need to pair with someone considered to be inferior in an attempt to bolster a diminished ego. AA meetings are filled with such stories; they are commonplace and considered to be only one of the many manifestations of this disease.

We have all heard the phrases "Male Menopause" and "Mid-Life Crisis." Anyone who has lived through this period knows it is not a myth. Hormonal changes at mid-life produce such traumatic disruption in some males that their personalities and resultant behavior undergo tremendous change also. Women do not have a monopoly on the "Change of Life."

For our study the reasons for the infidelity are immaterial. The reality of the situation is, it happened, and these wives were left with intense feelings of rejection, bitterness, loneliness, frustration and anger. Often that anger was directed more at The Other Woman than at the former spouse. There is a reason for this.

Martha, a gracious and sophisticated woman of fifty-five whose former husband is an alcoholic and drug addict, put it this way. "In those first years of our marriage my husband and I were deeply in love. We shared what to me will always be the most precious years of my life. We grew up together. We grew a family together. When that love is placed on a scale opposite his betrayal it does carry weight, and I do have compassion for him. I'm not the only one who lost a marriage. He lost one too. As far as his girlfriend is concerned my feelings for her are disgust and even hatred. I suppose that's why most of my anger has been directed at her."

It is important to understand that in order to heal we must give vent to our anger in whatever direction we find necessary. Remember, healing cannot occur until the true anger has been brought to the surface, worked through and let go. Following are some ideas on ways to do your venting against The Other Woman.

Let It Go

***Write a
Letter***
    A whole manuscript if need be. Pour every word, name and insult you feel onto that paper. Keep it in a notebook on your desk or dining room table and add to it daily—nightly—whenever you feel the need. Hold nothing back. When you're really brimming over, read it out loud. Scream it if it feels right. Then when you've purged yourself, close the notebook and physically walk away from it. Go to a window, or better still, outside, and look at whatever beauties of nature your particular setting offers: a beautiful landscape, a glorious sunset, a starry night. For at least a two-minute period, repeat an affirmation such as,

> Every minute of every day I grow in strength, understanding and forgiveness.

Cry if you need to; you'll feel better for it. Let the tears flow like a cleansing rain that washes away the dirt and makes the world fresh again. When you're finished you'll be ready to return to whatever you were doing before you opened your notebook. But before you do, pause for a moment and whisper to yourself some words of thanks for whatever blessings you have in your life: your health, your home, your food, your job, your children, your friends, your sanity. Then remember to congratulate yourself on completing one more exercise in healing.

"The Yellow Pages Yank"

This one requires the sacrifice of your Yellow Pages, the book your fingers do the walking through. Hopefully, it's a thick one. Hold the Yellow Pages in your lap and grasp several pages at once. Tear them out of the book by the handful. With each yank tell yourself that it's a handful of her hair. Snatch her bald-headed. Don't stop your tearing until the book is as bare as her head, then allow yourself a good laugh at how really ridiculous she looks now—something like a plucked chicken! If this isn't enough, move on to the next suggestion.

"The Yellow Pages Swing"

Find yourself a baseball bat. And another Yellow Pages. (Women going through divorce need lots of Yellow Pages!) Get a clear picture of her face before you, and mentally paint it on the cover. Lay the book down on a sofa or chair and literally pound the daylights out of it. Swing that bat with all the strength you can muster and don't stop until your arms are so tired you can't lift them again. If you've run out of Yellow Pages, sacrifice a pillow. One woman told me she had a pillow case on which she'd painted a replica of her rival's face. When she needed to vent she covered the pillow with this case and pounded her into oblivion. "I went through six pillow cases and four pillows before I got it out of my system," she told me proudly, "and it was worth every penny."

"The Lion"

Whether there's another woman or not, this exercise will be helpful as a venting/healing tool. You are encouraged to do this exercise often, although in the beginning you may not feel you are "ready" for it; as time passes you will find it easier to do.

There is a yoga posture that is particularly helpful in getting rid of negative emotions. It is called by a variety of names, but it is most commonly known as "The Lion." It is performed by assuming a kneeling position on the floor, knees together, sitting on your heels, hands atop your knees. Close your eyes and form a mental picture of whomever you are feeling angry toward. Bring the face in close so you can look deep into the eyes. Take a deep breath and raise your hands over your head, open your mouth, stick out your tongue, and bug your eyes. Now propel your body forward until your hands and knees are on the floor—as if you were pouncing on a prey. As you are doing this, roar from the depths of your gut. Pounce on that detestable face and pound it into the dust. Now rock back on your heels again, close your eyes, calm yourself with another deep breath or two and do it all again. Pick another face, or if you prefer, the same one—whoever is causing you anger or disharmony, anyone who at anytime in your life has hurt or angered you: your mother, father, ex-mate, third-grade teacher, yourself, any and all. Do this a total of three times. Do it with every bit of emotion you can muster. Your throat should be feeling strained by now, and your gut decidedly less full.

Now change your position so you are seated cross-legged on the floor. Rest your hands on your knees and once again close your eyes. Breathe deeply several times to quiet yourself. Now visualize a brilliant white light that slowly descends from above. It enters the crown of your head and rushes through your body, filling you with a beautiful, soothing, effervescent light. The light fills you with peace, with love. Take a deep breath and breathe in this peaceful beauty, allowing it to fill you completely. The white light gradually becomes larger, fuller, wider and wider until it reaches outward in a beautiful white arc, and you are the center of this glorious, healing light.

With your eyes still closed, off in the distance you see the crumpled forms the lion destroyed. Mentally raise up one of those forms, and slowly, gently bring it toward you. You can see the face now. The face is near enough to feel the warmth and beauty and peace of the white light. Slowly reach out your arms and bring the face nearer to the white light, nearer to you. Bring it into the light, into the beauty. Quietly, tenderly, hold it close in your embrace, and let it go. Now reach out again for the next form—whomever the lion destroyed—and repeat the healing. Do this three times. Remember, if the lion destroyed *you*, bring yourself back into the healing light; allow yourself to feel all the love and forgiveness and beauty. This is the part of you that needs healing, needs to feel loved. Be kind. Be generous. Be loving.

At the end of the final embrace, take another deep breath, then slowly open your eyes as you repeat,

I am healed. I am whole.

If you can accept that all men are indeed created equal—and we're talking now in the spiritual sense, not the physical—it is wise to remember that although these people are presently manifesting something you find distasteful, this in no way diminishes their spiritual nature. They are in spirit as the Creator created us all—perfect. It is the human side of their nature that is troubling you. That, of course, is what the above exercise is intended to help us understand, and with enough practice and sincere effort we *will* understand.

For some of us, one reaction to hurt is to seek revenge. Again, if we are being honest with ourselves, we will see that revenge is a reaction to an assault on our ego (not our spirit, for spirit is unassailable). Many of us have been witness to the fact that "what goes around comes around." In other words, the universal law of cause and effect takes care of all unsettled debts. At some time, at some place, retribution will be meted out. We don't have to do it and we don't have to wait until Judgment Day. Whatever debts are incurred on the physical plane will be paid off on the physical plane. Of course, no matter how understanding or forgiving we become, the human side of us would like to be there to see the lesson being learned. And often we are.

In addition to the suggestions mentioned above, you can utilize other "emergency" stress relievers—again depending on your own particular likes and needs. These are safety valves that will help get you through those moments of anger and panic.

Get Physical Exercise

Long walks may be helpful at other times, but when we are talking "emergency" that may not do it. What is recommended here is heavy exercise.

- Put on your video exercise disc and get a really good workout. This is one of the best forms for emergency relief because you are forced to pay attention to the instructor on the screen and ignore the harangue in your head.

- Several hard laps in the pool at as fast a pace as you can muster. Concentrate on your breathing as you swim. What you are aiming for is a state of real physical fatigue.

- Walk or run up and down the stairs, but you must count the steps. Counting helps you to concentrate on what you are doing instead of what you don't want to be thinking about. Visualize the numbers as you count them. Try Roman numerals: they require more concentration.

Do Something Creative

- Replant a shrub or small tree, or get your house plants together and replant them. Digging in the dirt and getting your hands in the earth is a terrific relaxer for many people. But remember to concentrate totally on what you are doing. Think only of the job at hand. Talk to your plants. Sing to them. It'll help you both.

- Rearrange the furniture, preferably in a way it hasn't been before. This will make you concentrate on the outcome of your project. The benefits of the physical exercise are obvious, but don't get carried away! Laid up in bed with a bad back is not on the agenda.

- Pull out your recipe book and whip up something brand new. Make sure it is something you've never tackled before, because that will take your complete concentration to follow the recipe. The more complicated the recipe the better. So what if there's nobody there to eat it? You can always freeze it, give it away, or invite somebody over!

- Go shopping. Forget about the price tags. Buy whatever it is you want. You can always return it later. Instant Gratification = Instant Therapy.

- If painting or drawing interests you, get out the old sketch pad and go to work. Some of the world's greatest masterpieces have been inspired by anger and created under stress.

If these ideas don't appeal, invent some of your own. This is another way of taking responsibility for yourself, and there's no better time to do that than now.

Exercises

The three steps in dealing with anger are:

1. Bring it out.

2. Deal with it.

3. Let it go.

However, before we can begin bringing it out, we must first recognize that the anger is there. We must be tuned into our inner workings enough so we can recognize anger for what it is and not call it by another name or, worse still, let it go unacknowledged. Take a few minutes to fill in the chart below. Review your past week and see what happened, how you felt, how you handled or didn't handle anger, and what you would do differently, if anything. Are you surprised we only have to look back a week? Most of us have occasion to get angry every day.

Incident	I felt...	I did...	I wanted to...	I wish I...

1. Looking at your chart, if you gave a passive answer under "I felt...," such as "nothing" or "not upset," and in retrospect you see the incident as clearly anger provoking, it may be beneficial to finish the following statement: When I deny that I am angry it is usually because:

From your chart you can gain some insight into how you handle/don't handle anger. Let's take a few steps backward to examine where these behavior patterns began. Remember, just because we are now carrying certain behavior patterns, we don't have to haul them around with us forever.

2. When I was a child and I got angry I used to:

3. As a child, when I expressed my anger in this way my caretakers reacted by:

4. Today when I am angry I usually:

5. Today the people around me usually react to my anger by:

6. One thing that always makes me angry is:

7. My anger is usually directed toward:
- ☐ myself
- ☐ others
- ☐ some unnamed source

8. I believe anger is a manifestation of ego and not of spirit.
- ☐ Yes
- ☐ No
- ☐ Sometimes

9. I am willing to acknowledge the dual facets of my nature; my humanity and my spirituality.
- ☐ Yes
- ☐ No
- ☐ Sometimes

10. I am comfortable in accepting both parts of my nature.
- ☐ Yes
- ☐ No
- ☐ Sometimes

Notes and Reflections

Love thy neighbor as thyself.

— Leviticus 19:18

Do unto others as you would have others do unto you.

— Luke 6:31

Chapter 4

Taking Charge

L ove thy neighbor as thyself." Obviously this famous passage is exhorting us to feel good things about our neighbor, while at the same time counseling us to feel good things about ourself. The Golden Rule encourages us to treat others as lovingly as we want to be treated (Matthew 7:12).

Loving ourselves is a natural state of being, but one we all too often resist. We tend to confuse self-love with selfishness. Selfishness (ego) is "me first"—me before you at the head of the line, me with the whole cake and you with none, me in the spotlight and you in the shadows.

Self-love (self-esteem/spirit) is acknowledging our equal role in all things, thinking of circles instead of lines, recognizing the abundance of life and knowing there is enough of everything for everyone. Self-love is being joyous that each of us has our own uniqueness and our own time to shine. Self-love is taking care of ourselves, taking charge of ourselves, being responsible for ourselves. It means doing whatever we need to do for the betterment of our physical, emotional and spiritual self.

Sometimes we tend to work on one area of our self—for example, the physical—and don't pay too much attention to the emotional or spiritual. However, what is fed to one part of our being affects the others. So if we are being physically good to ourselves, we are giving strokes to our emotional and spiritual well being, too.

For starters, let's take a look at our physical selves. What do we do to take good care of ourselves physically?

My personal regimen includes eating properly and getting enough sleep. I work regular hours. I take time out to play. I exercise. I don't go overboard on anything (especially mourning my loss and venting my anger). I practice moderation in all my activities. I work at being my "woman of tomorrow," and I treat myself to perks as often as possible.

Perks include bubble baths, soothing music to fall asleep to, intellectual conversation with friends on subjects that do not revolve around my marital situation. Treating myself to perks means having a good dinner at a nice restaurant, or walking along a deserted beach or driving through the countryside. It means doing anything else I can think of that brings me peace and joy.

One favorite perk which I developed during the early months following my divorce and which I continue even today, is buying myself a small bouquet of flowers each week. They can usually be found for as little as $2.00. So what if I am on a tight budget? So what if it means substituting hamburger for veal chops? I am worth it! Flowers brighten my spirit each time I look at them; veal chops brighten my palate for a few moments.

In addition to being good to myself in the zillions of ways I can think of right off the top of my head, one of the biggest gifts I can give myself is the pure joy of doing "for me" what I had previously allowed and expected others to do for me.

In my own case I had depended on my spouse to help me with the movement of food, both into and out of the house. He carried in the groceries; he took out the trash. Now these are not tasks we readily think of as "being good to myself," but being independent enough to do these simple things for myself gave me a tremendous sense of self confidence! And in those early months I was certainly in need of building confidence!

I recall very clearly one winter morning when the real meaning of "taking charge of myself" hit home. Actually it was akin to being struck by lightning, but in retrospect I realized I had learned a valuable lesson in caring for my own needs—also in building self-esteem. It happened like this.

It was a Sunday morning, and as I sipped my coffee I began creating a mental agenda of the day's activities: get the newspaper, replenish the car's windshield wiper fluid, do the laundry, buy a carton of sour cream, return three telephone calls, pay the bills. It seemed like a full day.

At that time I was living in an apartment, and while the rooms themselves were quite comfortable, the plumbing leaned toward archaic. In order to operate the washing machine, which was in the kitchen, it was necessary to take the extension hose from the washer and place it in the sink, since there were no drain facilities for the machine. My ex had been very helpful in working through this problem with me and had installed a long piece of plastic tubing onto the end of the hose so it would fit snugly into the garbage disposal and not pop out each time the water pumped through.

"Okay," I told myself, "get moving! Throw a load of wash in and go out for the morning paper and sour cream." I loaded the washing machine, carefully placing the hose and its extension into the sink, grabbed the gallon bottle of window washer fluid and headed downstairs.

It was a cold, blustery day. A light layer of snow covered everything. I slipped behind the steering wheel and started the engine; then, releasing the lever to the hood, I grabbed my bottle of blue and made my way to the front of the car. Other than on two occasions when my former mate had pointed out the various workings of the engine (which I quickly forgot), I'd never been "under the hood."

I gave a tug on the closed hood and nothing happened. A second similar motion achieved the same results. Ummm. Reluctantly, I removed my mittens and tried again. Still nothing. I went back inside the car and pulled again on the little lever marked "Hood." Returning to the front of the car I tried a fourth time. Maybe I was grabbing in the wrong place. I slipped my now frozen fingers down another inch or two and felt a slight protrusion. Ah! I gave a hearty tug. *Craaack!* "Good Lord what was that?" The hood still hadn't moved. I bent over and saw to my extreme consternation that I had broken my car. The grille was in two pieces. Being plastic, it had stiffened in the cold. When pressure was applied it snapped in two. I wiped the snow from my face and muttered a few unladylike words, most of which were directed at my ex. Reason had evaporated in the frigid air. This was definitely his fault!

Maybe I should go to the grocery store first and give the car a chance to warm up. The windshield wiper fluid could wait another ten minutes. I hauled myself back into the car, pitched the pieces of the grille into the back seat and headed for the store.

By the time I returned fifteen minutes later, the heat indicator was finally beginning to move. I gave a final yank on the lever marked "Hood" and with all of my control and determination in tow, headed again for the front of the automobile. This time I approached my task from a different perspective. I got down on my hands and knees, hooked my thumb up under what I knew to be the hood, stood up and yanked. The hood flew up, catching my chin as it went.

I picked myself up off the ground, fished the windshield washer bottle out from beneath the car where it had rolled and spent the next several minutes wiping blood from my chin while trying to understand the maniacal mind of the engineer who had designed the bottle cap. For starters, you either needed glasses (mine were upstairs) or an understanding of braille in order to get it open.

Ten minutes later I had completed my task. I could now handle anything the slush-filled highways of New England could throw at me.

"Well, this time was a learning experience," I counseled myself. "Next time it'll be a cinch!"

I trudged upstairs to my apartment, clutching the villainous bottle, the morning paper and my carton of sour cream.

As I closed the door behind me I had a sudden feeling of uneasiness. I glanced into the kitchen. Spuds, carrots, onion skins and bits of broccoli were flying through the air. A potato hit the wall and splattered. My understanding was instantaneous; there wasn't a doubt as to the source. It was last night's dinner. A few steps into the kitchen confirmed my suspicions. The washing machine was happily spewing garbage with every surge of its little pump. I had neglected to dump the garbage disposal. In addition to the leftovers, garbage-laced water covered the counter tops, the kitchen table, the refrigerator, the stove and the floor. I waded through the water and shut off the machine.

The way I looked at it, I had two options. I could either throw myself down and pound the floor with my fists, or I could get out the mop and towels and clean it up. Since I had no audience, I chose the latter.

Two hours later, things were looking up and I was feeling pretty good about "Taking Charge of the Situation."

In time I got a lot better about taking care of myself. I learned to look before leaping, to think things through a little more carefully (foresight had never been a strong point), and bit by bit I came to realize the gut-deep joy that comes with knowing, "I can get through life without a director!"

Many of our sisters who contributed to this book had similar stories to tell: locking themselves out of their homes, struggling with the mysteries of balancing a checkbook, holding down a first-time-ever job, being stranded at night on a deserted highway, or coping alone with a seriously ill child. In essence, the lessons were the same. Look at the situation and do whatever you feel needs to be done. Of course you're going to be wrong sometimes. Everyone is. But that doesn't mean you haven't learned a valuable lesson from your experience. Screwing something up the first time and then succeeding on subsequent tries happens to everybody. (Ask the toddler who is learning to walk!) I'll tell you one thing: I've never again broken a car grille.

And speaking of cars, the following is Felicia's story of her experience when buying a new one.

"Everyone I'd talked to told me not to go into an auto dealership showroom without a man on my arm. Even if I had to rent one. But I was one hundred percent convinced

I could do this on my own, and did not need a man to help me pick out an automobile.

"I walked into the dealer's showroom with my head held high and my calculator in my pocket—ready to wheel and deal. Before going in I knew precisely what I wanted and precisely what I was willing to pay.

"Three hours later I came out with my head spinning and a signed sales agreement in my purse. It had been a difficult battle, but I'd overcome the opposition—or so I thought. I'd only agreed to $300 more than I'd planned on. And what a nice salesman. He was new at his job; I was only his third sale. And the poor man had lost his daughter in an auto accident just a couple of years ago. *Oh brother!*

"The following day I was to go back to pick up the car and hand over the rest of the cash. However, when I returned the following day, my salesman was not present, but he had left another sales agreement for me to sign—$150 higher than the agreed-upon price—and left it in the hands of a true mathematical genius who could do really incredible things with numbers. This guy gave a whole new meaning to the words 'con game.'

"To put it bluntly, I was suckered in. By the time I got home the light was beginning to dawn, and my anger at having been taken was mounting. The more I thought about it, the madder I got. I was mad at the salesman, I was mad at the con man, I was mad at my ex—but most of all I was mad at myself!

"I didn't sleep that night and at nine o'clock the next morning I was on the phone to the general manager of the auto dealership. I made an appointment to see him that evening after work. At the meeting I produced both sales agreements, and asked him what he intended to do about it. I also mentioned such words as 'Better Business Bureau,' 'Detroit home office' and 'local newspapers,' and hinted at 'TV coverage.' I left his office with a $150 check in my hand and his utmost apology for the 'mix up.'

"The experience was not pleasant, but I had stood my ground and won. After the anger faded, I realized I'd been tested and passed. It felt good."

There is no doubt it is difficult having to make decisions on our own, when we have become so conditioned to talking things over with a partner. But the bottom line here is: Learn to Trust Yourself. One nice thing about that is—you will always have a partner who has your best interests at heart.

Exercises

As we reach understanding about the difference between selfishness and self-love, it is not unusual to change the way we look at certain things, even long-held views. To consider ourselves as worthless or little more than worms in the dust is an insult to our Creator. It's saying, "Hey God, what you created is junk!" Nothing could be further from the Truth. In Truth, you are the most important thing that ever happened. In Truth, you are a thought in the mind of God. The idea of worthlessness is self-demeaning, egocentric, and a denial of Truth. We are all our Creator's children; there are no stepchildren. We are equal; we are made in our Creator's image (Spirit), which is perfect. It's what we do in our physical form that gets us into trouble. Wallowing in worthlessness is as much against our Creator's wishes as running roughshod over our brother or sister. The Golden Rule to love our neighbors as ourselves promotes *self*-respect as much as respect for others.

1. In acknowledgment of my creation, I am willing to take charge of all facets of my being: spiritual, emotional, mental and physical.

☐ Yes

☐ No

☐ Partially

2. How have you nourished these various parts of yourself over the past week? Here are some possible examples.

• Spiritual: Prayer/meditation

• Emotional: Communion with another/ listening to inspirational tapes or talks

• Mental: Reading or discussing something that charged my mind

• Physical: Exercise (walking, jogging, dancing, aerobics, yoga)

3. Look back on some of your experiences (since the divorce/separation) that were opportunities for growth. List some of them here. Don't beat yourself up if you didn't seize the opportunity; just remember it, and prepare yourself for next time.

4. "Today I can look back on some of these experiences and find a grain of humor in them."

☐ Yes

☐ No

Explain:

5. Some of the good things about living alone— without a partner—are:

6. Some of the negatives about living alone—without a partner—are:

7. I can work on changing these negatives by:

8. When I trust myself, I am trusting my God/Higher Power/Love/
Creator/Universal Force. In order to learn to trust this helping/
loving energy more, I will:

- ☐ Silently state my problem to whatever name I call my
  Creator, and ask for help/guidance.
- ☐ Offer a daily prayer of "Thanks" for the good in my life.
- ☐ Remember to end each and every prayer with, "I will to
  will Your will."
- ☐ Read something every day (even just a line or two) that
  will enrich my spirit.
- ☐ Make "listening" to my Creator through meditation part of
  my healing program.
- ☐ Remember to pray for others (not asking what *I want* for
  them but for whatever the Creator knows is best for them.

Notes and Reflections

Notes and Reflections

It is possible that in changing the way we view a thing we may actually change the thing viewed.

— Author Unknown

Chapter 5

Alone vs. Lonely

T here is a difference between these two states: Being alone opens the passageway to inner peace; being lonely promotes anguish. Here is yet another choice to be made on your journey to emotional freedom.

For many, the demise of our marriage presents us with the first occasion ever to live entirely on our own. To be the only person living at this address can be...

Scary?

You bet!

A chance to pull the covers over your head?

One of the best!

An opportunity to grow spiritually?

A golden one!

What you do with this period—if you are fortunate enough to have it—will play a large role in determining who and what your future woman will be. If you're feeling tense or fearful about living solo for a while, it may help to remember that one of your rights as a citizen of this country is independence of spirit. Unfortunately, this is something many of us stuff in a drawer along with the marriage certificate. Think about it: freedom and independence of spirit! You now have the opportunity to dream anything you want to dream, to be anything you want to be. The only limitations are the ones you place on yourself. If you have gained nothing else from your divorce, believe me, you have gained this. Grasp it. Hold on to it. Grow with it. You are in charge of your show!

"But I'm afraid!" you cry. "I'm afraid to be alone!"

There are many people who live in fear—which is another way of saying there are many unhappy people. So how do we let go of the fear in order to see the opportunities?

By changing our attitude.

For a moment, let's take a look at the positive side of single living.

- You cook a meal when you feel like it.

- You clean up only after yourself.

- You visit and entertain when you want and whom you want.

- You watch the television programs you want to see. (Or you don't watch television at all!)

- You go to bed when you are ready.

- You come and go at any hour of the day you choose.

- You get involved in activities of your choice.

- You meet new people who add new dimensions to your life.

- You are no longer emotionally drained by an unhappy or unhealthy relationship.

- You take sole responsibility for your happiness.

Rest assured this list will grow as the days slip by.

All of the above are ways in which you will learn, minute-by-minute, hour-by-hour, just what it is that gives you pleasure.

"Oh, but I'm in such pain I can't believe I'll ever be happy again!" Yes, this is true—for however long you need it to be. Grieving, mourning, crying your guts out and pounding the pillow in rage and frustration, are part of the healing process; they're not things anyone wants to do, but they are necessary steps.

Now let's take an honest look at the negative side of single living.

- You're frightened at the prospect of being alone.

- You're concerned about money and whether you can make it on your own.

- You feel abandoned, betrayed and unprotected.

- You see yourself as unlovable—and unloving.

- You feel you need someone to care for and someone to care for you.

- You have no idea what you want to do with your life, and wonder if there really is a reason to go on.

- You are finding it nearly impossible to sleep or you are sleeping far too much.

- You are unable to swallow food—or you are gorging continually.

- You feel sexually frustrated and wonder if you'll ever have a tender, loving partner again.

- You want something to kill the pain: booze, drugs, a new man—something!

I'm sure you can add to this list.

Now let's go back over these lists with our eye on a different perspective—a change in attitude. Let's look again at the first list.

You cook a meal when you feel like it. We could look at this another way, of course. You can say, "Oh, there isn't really any sense in spending all that time in the kitchen.

I have no one to cook for, no one who appreciates my efforts."

You clean up only after yourself. We could translate this into, "It takes so little time to do the housework now; I have too much time on my hands."

You visit and entertain when you want and whom you want. We could construe this as, "I feel awkward visiting or entertaining married friends. I feel like a fifth wheel."

Take the rest of the list and we could come up with negatives for each one. I once shared a weekend with a woman who greeted a magnificent sunrise with the comment, "Oh Lord, another dawn. I wonder what will go wrong today?" And you can bet it did! That's the victim mentality at work again. The point, of course, is that the positive perspectives are a matter of attitude.

Now let's take a look at our second list and see how or what we can change.

You're frightened at the prospect of being alone. It's important to examine what exactly you are afraid of. Are you frightened at the thought of an intruder? Homes with males in residence are broken into nightly! Are you afraid you won't be able to take care of your home by yourself—fix the plumbing, make repairs, shovel the snow, whatever? Then this is a perfect opportunity to either learn new skills or otherwise put your creative processes to work. Maybe a move is in order! Maybe sharing chores with a neighbor will work, "This week we'll cut your lawn and next week we'll do mine." What one of you doesn't know how to do, the other may. Whatever it is that frightens you should be honestly addressed. Only then can you find an honest and workable solution. You need to ask yourself, "Am I afraid to be alone because I'm frightened of my own company?" It's not all that unusual to feel frightened at meeting someone, and many of us who have given too much to our marriage, invested our energies in our partner and neglected ourself, are frightened at the prospect of getting reacquainted with Number One. Peace of mind can only be found through making peace with yourself, and solitude is where that happens.

You're concerned about money and whether you can make it on your own. If you've never been responsible for handling money or keeping within a budget, this is your chance to learn a valuable lesson, one that will serve you throughout the remainder of your life. Figure out what it's going to cost you to live and find a way to get the funds—a job, a second job, a roommate. Perhaps reducing expenses is the answer: cheaper housing, lunch bags instead of cafes, car pooling, selling something. Everyone can reduce expenses with a little ingenuity. The satisfaction that comes at the end of the month when you find the bills paid and know you have done this on your own, is a building block of self-confidence.

You feel abandoned, betrayed and unprotected. Let's face reality here. Just how much "protection" did you really have from the man who betrayed you, from the man who abandoned you either physically or emotionally? Zero! That was illusion. The only real protection you will ever have is the protection you give yourself, which is as it should be. Protecting you is your job. You are your responsibility. Children receive protection from adults; adults protect themselves. If protecting yourself is a new experience for you, I can assure you it will be a rewarding one.

You see yourself as unlovable—and unloving. Just because your former mate no longer loves you does not mean that no one else does. Think about this. Is there no one—not even a parent, a child, a sibling, a friend—who loves you? Of course there is! What your ex not loving you *does* mean is that, for the moment, there is not a man in your life. That is a far cry from being unlovable.

And what about the unloving part? Is there truly no one whom you love? You know this is not true. Love has many facets, and just because right now there isn't a lover in your life does not mean that you cannot experience other types of love. As a matter of fact, this is a wonderful opportunity

65

to do just that. When we are concentrating heavily on an intimate relationship—especially when we are trying to salvage it—we expend a great deal of energy and consequently neglect other areas of our "love life. You now have an opportunity to explore, and renew, those other love relationships.

You feel you need someone to care for and someone to care for you. Shakti Gawain, in her book *Reflections in the Light*, said it better than anyone I know:

> When we finally give up the struggle to find
> fulfillment outside of ourselves, we have nowhere
> to go but within. It is at this moment of total
> surrender that the light begins to dawn. We
> expect to hit bottom, but instead we fall through
> a trap door into a bright new world. We have
> rediscovered the world of our spirit.

Self-discovery is an exhilarating experience, an incomparable adventure. In addition, few things aid the building of self-esteem quite as much as "standing on your own two feet"—being a free and functional adult human being. As our spirituality strengthens and grows we will come to realize that each of us, each human being, has her own unique spirit. Your spirit is something that was entrusted to you by the Creator. If the Creator had intended you to have responsibility for someone else's spirit, you would have been given that spirit. But the Creator didn't intend that; the Creator gave you your own spirit. Therefore, since your spirit is the one entrusted to your care, it follows that it is your job to take care of *your* spirit first.

You have no idea what you want to do with your life, and you wonder if there really is a reason to go on. Ah! If this applies to you, then here is a real opportunity for an attitude change. If you saw your marriage as the end-all, your reason for living—and many of us did—then looking at marriage in a different way will undoubtedly provide enlightenment. Is marriage a goal or is it a way of living? An intimate partnership should not be our reason for living; it is a life-style. There are many life-styles. If you believe your *raison d'etre* is to be married you need to take a look around. "What's it all about, Alfie?" Why am I on this planet? What is the meaning of my existence? Do I have some business to take care of here? Do I have some lessons to learn? Ages of sages have pondered these questions, and nobody has ready answers. However, when you do question—and continue to question—I assure you the answers you find will not include marriage. You are not alive for the sole purpose of being married.

You are finding it nearly impossible to sleep, or you are sleeping far too much. Both reactions are due to the fear, the strangeness, the newness of your situation, and to the cacophony going on inside your head. If sleeplessness is the problem, there are several things you can try—one so elemental it's easily overlooked. If you are truly physically tired, your chances for a restful sleep are greatly improved. If you've run yourself through an emotional wringer all day, your chances for sleep are almost nil. Relaxation tapes such as the sound of gentle rain, the peaceful roll of the surf, the soothing chime of temple bells, or some of the self-hypnosis tapes are excellent relaxers. Reading or television may help to some degree because the goal is to get your mind off your problems and centered on something else so you can relax. If you are sleeping too much, recognize that this is a sign of depression and the means by which you are trying to escape the reality of your current situation. I suggest you talk it over with your doctor. My physician prescribed an anti-depressant which I used for about six weeks until I was able to reestablish my normal sleeping patterns.

You are unable to swallow food, or you are gorging continually. Emotional shock usually does one of two things to people. We either drop several pounds suddenly, or we pile them on. Since your physical well-being is as much of a concern now as your emotional health, it is important to take care of this as quickly as possible. For many of us, food equates with love. We don't feel loved—so we don't eat. Or we crave love to an unhealthy degree—so we gorge. Realizing that what is happening to your body is a direct result of your emotional state will point you in the right direction. Here again it becomes important to look at the future. Ask yourself, "What kind of woman will I be tomorrow? What will that woman look like tomorrow?" The nourishments you give yourself today—your thoughts, your prayers, your food—are laying that foundation. Discipline under stress is not easy; however, it is necessary.

You feel sexually frustrated, and you wonder if you'll ever have a tender, loving partner again. How much importance you placed on the sexual portion of your marriage relationship pretty well determines the degree of frustration you are apt to feel now. If sex played a major role and your partner was unfaithful, your feelings of rejection and frustration can be quite acute.

There are several ways to handle sexual frustration. An obvious one is masturbation. However, while you may be able to relieve the tension in your body, this does not answer the need for a tender, loving partner.

Another obvious answer is to find a new partner. Again, you may release bodily tension, but if you are being honest with yourself you know a casual relationship does not fill the need for a tender, loving partner. Sex is not love. It can be an expression of love when accompanied by loving emotions. It can also simply be a means of relieving sexual energy. The key to health is knowing the difference.

That partner you are looking for (if you decide that is really what you want) will come along, but only after you have done your work on healing yourself. Beware if love appears too early on your horizon! However, it is important to acknowledge your sexual feelings and not deny them— noticing a nice pair of buns walking down the street, an attractive bared chest at the beach, a "Hey Baby!" look from across the room at a cocktail party. Experiencing your sexuality, keeping in touch with it, is healthy. You don't necessarily have to act on it. Just remember it is there; it is a part of you. It is a part of being alive. We will take a deeper look at this issue later (chapter 8).

In the meantime, another positive way to handle sexual frustration is through vigorous exercise. Our pent-up energy is released and the resultant fatigue promotes sleep. But here again, let's remember the importance of the mind. Sex, like every other physical urge, begins in the mind. When you learn to control your thoughts, you learn to control all aspects of your life.

You want something to kill the pain: booze, drugs, a new man—something! Know that all pain begins in the mind—very often, the subconscious mind. Everything that happens to you is first a thought before it manifests into the physical. Therefore, gaining control of your mind's thought process by bringing your subconscious thoughts into your conscious mind is the key to your release from pain. Then, changing your attitude about your situation, being willing to look at it in another way, determining within your own mind and heart that you do want to be happy and that you do deserve happiness, is the way out. Booze, drugs, a new man before you're ready—all are tools we may be tempted to use, but they won't work. Drugging your body to the point where your mind cannot function cures nothing. Trying to find happiness and fulfillment through a man, your children, or anyone else doesn't work because your happiness doesn't lie with them; it lies within you. Right now it may be locked within you, but you are the only one who has the key.

The single life-style is a different life-style. Naturally, there will be things you miss from the married life-style, but the sooner you begin letting go of the past and begin appreciating all the good in the present, the sooner you will heal. Keeping busy—keeping your hours filled with activities and people you enjoy—is an effective tool for beating the blues. As you readjust and settle into your new life, there will come a time when you will look forward to your evening or weekend—alone. The day will come (promise!) when you will walk through your door, kick off your shoes, throw the lock and sigh, "Thank heaven I don't have to talk to another living soul this evening! Thank heaven I can just be alone!"

You'll know then that you have begun your journey into self-discovery. You'll know then that the most intimate communion you have with your Higher Power comes only in those moments when you are alone with your Higher Power. You'll know then that the word "alone" means something quite different from what you had known it to mean before. You'll know then the precious meaning of "solitude."

Exercises

It is important to differentiate between being alone and being lonely because the two are vastly different, though sometimes confused. Being alone offers an opportunity for spiritual fulfillment; being lonely breeds a sense of emptiness.

1. I understand the state of loneliness as being:

2. When I reach back into my past, I remember my first encounter with loneliness. (This may have been a personal experience, or it may have happened to someone else.) Explain.

3. After reading the following statements, circle the number that best relates to you.

     1 = always
     2 = usually
     3 = sometimes
     4 = hardly ever
     5 = never

I feel lonely.	1 2 3 4 5
I am afraid to be alone.	1 2 3 4 5
I enjoy being alone.	1 2 3 4 5
I talk to myself when I am alone.	1 2 3 4 5
I pray when I am alone.	1 2 3 4 5
When I am by myself, I play the bad scenes over and over.	1 2 3 4 5

4. I see people who I know are lonely as:

5. I see people who spend time alone as:

6. I understand that a true shift in attitude is all that is required to move from loneliness to aloneness.

☐ Yes

☐ No

7. If you checked "No" above, explain what you believe is required.

8. I understand that the well-rounded person requires both solitude and companionship.

☐ Yes

☐ No

☐ Maybe

9. What other people think of me is:
- ☐ Very Important
- ☐ Somewhat Important
- ☐ Sometimes Important
- ☐ Barely Important
- ☐ Not Important

10. When people know I live alone they probably think I am:
- ☐ Courageous
- ☐ Unable to keep a man
- ☐ Deprived of sex
- ☐ Pathetic
- ☐ Well-adjusted
- ☐ Gay
- ☐ In charge of my life
- ☐ Lonely
- ☐ Dysfunctional
- ☐ Leading a wild life
- ☐ Strange
- ☐ Other (Explain:)

Notes and Reflections

If I hadn't believed it, I wouldn't have seen it.

— Burt Hotchkiss

Chapter 6

Love and Hate—
The Two-Edged Sword

Part of the human dilemma is that although we yearn to share our lives, our wishes and dreams, and our innermost feelings with that one special someone who will understand us totally, in truth we live in a private, secret world. To a large degree this is a world of illusion. This private world is shaped by our thoughts, emotions and experiences. What is real for one is not necessarily real for someone else.

This truth became apparent to me during my sojourn as a newspaper reporter. While interviewing people at the scene of an accident, I would inevitably get as many versions of what had happened as people I spoke with. Six people, six views. Oh, there were similarities, but each person had a separate, unique story of the event. Inevitably, one person had seen something that the others had not seen. On more than one occasion I was reminded of that game we played as children, the one where everyone sits in a circle and one person writes down a secret, then whispers it to the next person, and that person whispers what she heard to the next and so on until the story has traveled around the circle. The last one in the circle then says aloud what she has heard, and when the initiator reveals what she had really written everyone doubles over with laughter because the two stories are so vastly different.

In time I came to realize the reasons behind people's different realities. Each of us is at any given moment the sum total of our past experiences. No one has the exact same history as another. Even Siamese twins view the world from different perspectives. How often we hear someone say, "I raised all my children in the same home with the same set of values, but look how different they've turned out." This uniqueness is one of the things that separates us from our fellow human beings. Although we are all on the same planet, in the same space and time, our view of the world is never exactly the same as anyone else's. And this is also true of our view of love.

For most of us the experience of "falling in love" is such a powerful emotion, so intricately laced with so many other emotions and experiences, we are often convinced that no one else ever felt this way. To a great extent this is true. Not even the person with whom we share this wondrous experience views it in exactly the same way—and this ultimately, inevitably leads to discord. "But if I do this for you because I love you, why won't/don't you do the same for me?" Then we come to realize that the other person doesn't experience "love" in exactly the same way or to exactly the same degree as we do. We soon come to realize there is a positive and a negative side to love. Often (if not always) both sides operate simultaneously. The "oneness" we imagined at the onset of the relationship dims, and we are left feeling disappointed, isolated, alone. The object of our adoration is, after all, separate from ourself. This disillusionment introduces the negative side of love. How often we lament, "He just isn't the person I thought he was!" Of course he isn't! How could he be? You made him up! In part at least, he is a creation of your own mind. You saw what you wanted to see. Should he be blamed, or should we? Is there reason to blame at all? It is a little unfair to point a scornful finger at someone else for not fulfilling our own very private dream.

Because our expectations are precisely that—expectations—we are bound (doomed) to be disappointed. Our beloved will not always behave as we want (need) him to behave. Does this mean we shun love in order to keep from being disappointed? Not at all! But it does mean we need to realign our thinking about love, to understand that every human relationship offers opportunities for growth and learning. If there were no obstacles to overcome, no stretching of ourselves to understand the other's needs, no give and take or compromise, we would not learn or grow. Each human relationship is a unique relationship, and at a spirit level we come together for the purpose of growth and learning. Whether we choose to accept that challenge or let it go is up to us. Of course, the ideal love relationship is one in which the two people grow together while maintaining their separate identities. *On Golden Pond* was written about real people. Here was a father and daughter who loved and hated and accepted each other's individuality.

There is an old saying, and like most old sayings, it has a ring of truth. "One man's junk is another man's jewel." Take a stroll around a flea market or an antique store or even the junk yard, and you'll see what I mean. We see exactly what we want to see, and further, we believe exactly what we want to believe. Every war, every argument, every dispute and disagreement, stems from the fact that each of us has our own view of how things are or how we think they should be. This is especially true where love is concerned.

When we admit to ourselves that the person we love is something different than we had imagined, a process is set in motion.

1. We feel disappointed, perhaps even cheated.

2. We become disillusioned.

3. We get angry.

4. We harbor resentment.

5. We experience hatred.

This is the process that occurs each and every time we love. It is the negative side of love, the other edge of the sword. Even the most innocent love, that between a mother and newborn, is subject to the same process. In the beginning everything is roses, but after the third all-night session both participants become disenchanted. Mom is desperate for sleep, and her patience is wearing thin; Junior is furious that his needs are not being met and is letting the world know about it. The process is a natural one. Love does not exist without hate.

During the divorce and its aftermath, many of us become consumed with hatred for our former spouse. After all, we say to ourselves, how could we possibly love someone who has behaved in such a manner? The reality is we have not let go of the love, and we are manifesting only the negative aspects of the emotion because that is all we are willing to admit we feel. It is well to remember that hate binds two people together every bit as much as love. Hating the person you divorce is as self-defeating as continuing to love him in the same way you once loved him. The marriage is over; the relationship must change or end, if you are to be free to get on with your life. Can you consider developing a friendship with your former mate—a more casual, less intense relationship? If this is not possible for you, then total detachment may be the answer. Either new way of relating serves the purpose of releasing the love/hate and allowing new feelings—or no feelings—to take its place. Love has many faces.

I've always found it curious that the French language does not have a word for "like." Perhaps it is because the French are such a passionate people. They "love," they "cherish," they "adore," but they do not "like." We English speaking people are more fortunate in that we can find a nesting place for something a little less invested than "love."

But how do we change those feelings we once had into something else—or nothing else? Is there a magic formula? Oh, how we wish there was! In undertaking this venture it is well to remember that love is a choice; it is something we choose (at some level) to do. And not loving is also a choice. Uncoupling does not happen overnight, any more than real loving occurs in a lightning flash. Uncoupling is done slowly, carefully, consistently. It is done with your mind—your disciplined mind, your persistent, controlled thought process. You begin by thinking about this other person in a different way. You stand outside the relationship and look at it from a different perspective, and when you have decided upon the results you wish to attain—a total detachment, a casual friendship, whatever—you begin to plan how you will achieve this. You do this in the same way you analyzed what kind of woman you want to be in the future and made your plans to become that woman. You lay your plans; you discuss it with your counselor; you go to the meetings that will help you gain strength and momentum in that direction. You join organizations that will give support, and you program yourself daily with cassette and video tapes. You role-play. You design scenes in your head of what you will say and how you will act when you speak with your former mate. You write and memorize the script of what you want to say and how you want to say it. And you deal with it in your own time. You do not allow yourself to be pushed or taken off-guard. Your guard is always up because you are in a position of vulnerability until you are in control of your thought processes and therefore in control of your behavior. This is your design. This is your play. This is your decision. This is your responsibility.

Again, it will be helpful to take a look into the future, just as you did when deciding what kind of woman you want to be after this is behind you.

If you have children still in school, pause for a moment to consider their graduation day. Visualize the event. How would you like it to "play"? Will your ex be there? Will the day be a happy, relaxed celebration centered around your child, or will it be filled with rancor, trepidation and sarcasm? Will your son or daughter be running between parents seated at opposite ends of the auditorium, trying to keep everyone happy? What about your child's wedding day? Will this be a day of joy unshadowed by ghosts of the past, or will it be a day you look forward to with dread? You do have a choice.

But what if he won't play? What if he wants a totally different relationship with you—or no relationship? Face it—you cannot control his actions or emotions. But you are in charge of your own. Go about your merry way and stick to your game plan. In most cases, and almost certainly when the husband is the initiator of the divorce, he will eventually be willing to meet you on your turf. The reason being guilt. I'm not suggesting you should play on that guilt, not for one minute; but I am saying you are in the driver's seat if you choose to be in the driver's seat, and with persistence you will achieve your goal. Successful living is not simply resisting life's problems; successful living is *handling* life's problems.

And always, always, keep in mind that no matter what the situation, you do have a choice. The mind controls the body; the mind controls the emotions. Make up your mind as to what you want the outcome to be, and stick to it.

Exercises

Down all the corridors of time, human beings have asked the same two basic questions, and we still ask them today:

1. Where do I find food?

2. Where do I find love?

We need to nourish both our body and our spirit. Deprived of either we wither and die, which makes the loss of love so terrifying. At a gut level, we are afraid we will never find love again, and that we will die without it. In times of crisis we are apt to forget that love is everywhere, that love surrounds us.

Love is literally a unique experience. Each of us experiences it in our own unique way; each of us expresses it uniquely. And each of us throughout our lifetime sees love in a variety of faces.

1. Using the chart below, describe how you feel about the many faces of love in your life.

Love is...					
feeling...	with my spouse.	with my parents.	with my kids.	with my friends.	with my Creator.
pure					
pain					
happy					
free					
selfish					
giving					
peaceful					
chaotic					
changing					
constant					

2. The opposite of love is hate. (There is a right or wrong answer, so don't be too hasty.)

☐ True

☐ False

Love and hate are two sides of the same sword. Love is the positive expression, and hate the negative one. As long as either of these emotions exists, there is at some level a need or desire to be connected to this person. It is only when we let go of both of these emotions that we are truly free of the relationship. The correct answer then is "False." The opposite of love and hate is indifference.

3. When someone stops loving me or withdraws love from me I feel:

4. When someone stops loving me or withdraws love from me I react by:

5. When my marriage ended, my love for my spouse:

☐ Died

☐ Changed

☐ Remained the same

6. When I realized my marriage was over, I felt:

7. In retrospect I see that my marriage was:

☐ Relatively happy

☐ Miserable

☐ Other (Explain:)

8. I confuse anger with hate:

☐ Yes

☐ No

☐ Sometimes

9. When I hate someone, I have difficulty talking about it.

☐ Yes

☐ No

☐ Sometimes

10. When I love someone, I have difficulty talking about it.

☐ Yes

☐ No

☐ Sometimes

11. I see unconditional love as loving someone's spirit while being nonjudgmental of what they are manifesting physically, mentally and emotionally.

☐ Yes

☐ No

☐ Unsure

Notes and Reflections

Enslavement is not in the bondage, but rather in the acceptance of it.

— Rabbi Arthur Gilbert

Chapter 7

Being Good to Yourself, Being Good to Him

When we make a commitment to a cause, to an ideal, or to another person, we make a statement publicly and personally that we are where we are, doing what we are doing, because this is what we have chosen to do, because this is where we have chosen to be. Of course we can change our minds, which is why people change jobs, drop out of school, move to another location, get divorced, and make any number of other changes in their life pattern. This too is commitment—commitment to our inner urgings.

However, when we feel this urge to make changes, when we know that making some change is what we truly want—or need—to do, and we resist, we have relinquished our commitment, we have given up our freedom of choice and accepted bondage in its place. We make myriad excuses, all of which boil down to fear—fear of making a mistake, fear of change, fear of hurting ourselves or someone else, fear of the unknown.

One of the greatest fears human beings have is the fear of abandonment. This fear is universal, touching each and every person on this planet. We are terrified of being abandoned, and we all experience abandonment to one degree or another. We experienced it as infants when we awoke crying in the night and no one was there to comfort us. Even if someone eventually came and held us in warm, loving arms, it was too late; the sense of abandonment took place before our first cry, when we awakened to find we were alone. We had already convinced ourselves that something "outside" us was necessary to our well-being. It is a belief repeatedly reinforced over the years, until it is so ingrained in our adult psyche that we are convinced it is true.

We are convinced that we need someone outside ourselves to fill us, and we are equally convinced that at some point in time, we will again be abandoned. The Truth is, everything we need for our emotional well-being is already inside us. In Truth, we need nothing else. In Truth, there is nothing anyone can give us that we do not already have. The mystery is to find this wonderful well of wholeness and peace that lies within. As long as we continue to search for fulfillment where it cannot be found—in another person, another location, another job, another anything—we are setting ourselves up for pain and disappointment. The proverbial bluebird of happiness does live in our own backyards—more specifically, in our own beings.

We said earlier that ego is to the body what self-esteem is to the spirit. If you have accepted that you are indeed a being with a dual nature, then you have probably experienced your ego and your spirit working more or less simultaneously, almost as if two separate people were living inside you, each pulling in a different direction. Although these two parts of our nature concern different parts of our lives, both are necessary for survival. Some people concentrate so heavily on one part that they quite literally deny the existence of the other. To deny either is to deny a part of your reality.

I often think of these two parts of myself as the angel on one shoulder and its counterpart on the other. One will say, "Oh come on, Elaine, have another dish of ice cream, drink, cigarette, whatever," while the one on the other side counsels, "You know this is not good for you; this is not in your best interest." This is a continuing battle we all face.

Ego, whose concerns are for the body, emotions and personality, maintains that if someone else spoke or acted differently, if some external circumstance were changed, all would be well. According to Ego's view, everything is outside of us and either contributes to our well-being or detracts from it.

Spirit, on the other hand, is concerned with our higher self and views the body as a vehicle of communication. Spirit is concerned with what is going on inside and says, "I have total responsibility for what happens to me, for my actions, emotions and feelings. Nothing outside myself—my Spiritual Self—is of any real consequence." As long as we are in this world, this dilemma will continue. It is part of material existence. However, we can choose which part of our nature we listen to at any given moment, remembering that the emotionally and mentally healthy are those who heed both and who have successfully integrated their ego and their spirit.

"Mentally and emotionally healthy!" "At peace with oneself and the universe!" What an enviable state to be in! But rather than sit back and envy someone who has achieved this ideal position, let's take a look at a few of those who have it and see how they got there.

Charlotte is an attractive divorced woman with a superior IQ. She reared four children and reentered the workforce when the youngest entered school. She was past fifty when her husband of twenty-three years told her he no longer loved her. There wasn't anyone else, he said. It was just that the flame of love had died. Charlotte was devastated. She still loved her husband, and although the relationship was not perfect, they had, in her opinion, built a comfortable life together.

Much earlier, Charlotte had "accepted" the fact of her husband's periodic drinking bouts and had, on the surface at least, learned to live with it. However, the emotional trauma she was experiencing now was something she needed help with, and when her spouse declined to join her in marriage counseling, she decided to try Al-Anon.

"It was the turning point for my relationship as well as for me personally," she recalls. "My growth was gradual, but steady. I learned, as so many others have learned, that living in an alcoholic home places a terrible burden on everyone in that home: spouse, children, parents—even the pets feel the effects of the disease.

"I came to see and understand the role I was playing, that of the enabler, and how my attempts to control everything in my life, my childrens' lives and my husband's life was a part of *my* disease. Of course the thing that needed controlling was the very thing I couldn't control—my husband's compulsion to drink.

"Since alcoholism is a progressive disease, my husband's mental, moral, emotional, and physical condition continued on a downward spiral, and since I was in a self-help program my health began to improve.

"It took another five years before things came to a head, but I know now that divorce was inevitable. Although we had stayed together and tried to maintain some semblance of a marriage, he was actually far too ill to be capable of participating in a relationship. Eventually, he started having an affair, and although I struggled on for another two years, we finally divorced.

"The day I reached my 'bottom' and told my husband to leave, he walked from our door to 'the other woman's' door and moved in.

"At first I was terribly bitter toward him and toward this woman who had pretended to be my friend. Then he began calling every week or so and writing long, plaintive letters about how much he missed our marriage, our home, our life together. By this time I'd been in the Al-Anon program long enough to understand that this was pure and simple manipulation. Oh, he missed his old life, all right, there was no doubt about that, but like everyone who suffers from chemical dependency he could think only of himself and his own 'needs'. His continual mood swings and roller coaster 'changes of heart' were part of his disease.

"Many of my friends and all of my family were astounded—and alarmed—that I would even keep in contact with him, but I saw it in a very different light. I saw a man who was in a desperate state, not only physically but emotionally, mentally and morally as well. Should I completely turn my back on someone I had loved for the major portion of my life simply because he was too sick to control what he was doing with his life? Although my feelings had changed and I no longer loved him as I once had, I still had a great love for him spiritually. No matter what he was manifesting on a physical [ego] level, the inner light of the man, his spirit, was what I continued to love, and I am sure will always love.

"The growth I have experienced, the changes that have taken place inside me, are amazing even to me. I can only say that when I stood back and looked at the ruins of my marriage, I made up my mind then and there I was going to survive. I was determined to carve out a rich and mean-ingful life for myself. One of the immediate benefits was the tremendous sense of relief that comes when you are no longer living with an active alcoholic. I hadn't realized the incredible stress I had been under until I was free of it.

"From the moment we separated I began filling my life with activities and friends I truly enjoyed. I spent a lot of time developing my spiritual nature, learning forgiveness, learning to let go. The pain and desperation gradually slipped away and was replaced by compassion and accep-tance. I think that word "acceptance" is the key. Through understanding I was finally able to accept what had hap-pened to my husband, to understand his illness instead of deny it. I learned to accept him as he is today and not to continually try to force him to be the man he used to be. I may not like who he has chosen to be, but that is his decision.

"Eventually I reentered the social scene and began dating. Within that first year I came to realize how precious and important my freedom and independence truly are. I found it a great boost to my ego to have men telephoning and asking me to dinner, dancing, the theater, walks in the woods. I no longer had to prod and cajole someone into accompanying me. In truth I really began enjoying my new life.

"It's been four years since my marriage ended, and the time I've spent living alone and really getting to know myself, learning to nurture and love myself, has been the most profound experience of my life. I don't know if many people will understand when I say that I now know how to love myself. And I do love myself. I don't think I could have attained this if I'd stayed in the marriage. And speaking of marriage, I'm contemplating a new one. This time I am looking at it through very different eyes and with very different expectations. I no longer depend on anyone else to give me my happiness. That's something I give myself. Nor am I anticipating giving my new husband happiness. That's his domain. What we can give each other is companionship, caring, emotional support, trust, and honesty. For me, that's what love is all about. I'm a very grateful woman for having had two loves in my life. Not everyone is that fortunate."

Charlotte's face and entire being fairly glow with an inner peace that is almost a visible light. How did she attain this? What makes her different from those who do not have this inner sanctuary of oneness with her higher self? She has consciously striven to integrate both parts of her nature. She put her ego aside and listened to her higher nature when her husband's illness drove him to do things she knew were against his spiritual nature. She chose to love him spiritually rather than physically, and she found that love to be more satisfying than the ego-centered love they had once shared. She also listened to her own ego and appeased it by proving to herself that she was still a desirable woman. Charlotte is a woman at peace with herself because she is also at peace with others. In her own words, "I take quite seriously the words from the Bible that exhort us to love thy neighbor as thyself. The trick is to love yourself first, because only then do you have the tools required to love someone else."

Kathy is another woman whose life shines with that inner peace we are all searching for, and while her story is different from Charlotte's, there are important similarities.

Kathy's marriage lasted thirty years. During that time her husband turned the small family business his parents had started into a multi-million-dollar corporation. Kathy worked alongside her husband in a supportive role in the business as well as in the home.

"There was never any doubt in anyone's mind," Kathy relates, "about who was in charge. Ron is very much a take-charge person, and I've always been more than a little passive, so that was fine with me. I've always had a problem with handling responsibility, which made me a good second mate, I guess.

"Ron and I met right after high school, married within a year, and immediately began raising a family. We have one son and two daughters. We had a good marriage for a long time. Ron was away from home a lot, but that was okay. I enjoyed the time alone and Ron wasn't a playboy. Oh, he's handsome enough, but he's just not the cheating type.

"Our troubles began when the kids started leaving the nest and I hit menopause. It seemed that overnight I put on a tremendous amount of weight and went from a size eight to a fourteen. It bothered me a lot and I tried every diet known to man. Ron made it apparent that it bothered him, too. He began making unkind remarks about it, which only tended to diminish my already lowered self-image.

"Gradually, we began to go in different directions. I realized that money and status were becoming increasingly more important to Ron, while I was beginning to get in touch with my spiritual nature. I became involved in a small business with a friend I'd known for several years. Ron was furious. He complained I was spending too much time pursuing my interests. The break came one afternoon when I walked in the door and found Ron's suitcases sitting in the front hall. He said he needed to live by himself for awhile. A week later he told me he wanted a divorce. I felt as if my whole world had ended.

"The divorce took nearly a year because of the financial arrangements, but during that time we continued to see each other periodically for dinner and that kind of thing. I kept thinking, hoping, he would come to his senses and realize what he was giving up. That never happened. About three months after the divorce was final, he met someone and within six weeks they were married.

"It took a long time to put my life together again. It seemed I had lost everything: my husband, my role in the business, the support of my children—they were living their own lives and reluctant to even address what had happened to their parents' marriage.

"The small business I had started with my friend closed down when I'd pulled out in an effort to pacify Ron. I felt completely set adrift. I felt I had nothing and couldn't see

91

any reason to go on. In a last-ditch effort to save myself I began counseling sessions. I recall very well the day my therapist said to me, 'Despite all the apparent reasons for my various clients' problems, the underlying cause in almost every case is lack of self-esteem, which, at a deeper level, translates to not being in touch with the spiritual side of their own nature.' She went on to say that attempting to heal the effect without considering the cause is like putting a Band-Aid on a three-foot laceration. It's a stopgap, far from being a cure.

"Eventually, I began rebuilding my self-esteem, and ventured out into the business world again. I went into partnership with another friend and bought a small gift shop. It was tough going for the first few years, but things are fine now. We're going to make it, and for me the personal rewards have been tremendous.

"So I guess what you could say about my story is that I began looking inward for peace instead of 'out there some-where.' It has been seven years since my divorce. Ron and I are okay with each other now. We are not the best of friends; we have gone our separate ways. But we do talk on the phone now and then, and whenever something of a family nature comes along we see each other.

"A lot of people have asked me if I have forgiven him, and from my new perspective on life, I find that almost amusing. In order to forgive there would first have to be judgment, and that is something I'm trying not to do. I don't think anyone has the responsibility of judging anyone else. That's something each of us should do for ourselves—and only for ourselves. I no longer have to make accommodations for Ron in my life, nor does he have to do so for me. We each have changed direction, and that's okay. I'm glad Ron and I had a life together, but I wouldn't change what I have now for anything!"

Exercises

From the moment we enter this world of form, we sense a need for "something outside ourselves" to nourish us. As we grow older this belief becomes more deeply embedded in our minds until it is not even questioned—that is, until we are confronted by a crisis. When we are under pressure, when our backs are to the wall, we begin to look for peace and fulfillment in the only place it can be found: inside ourselves.

As you answer the questions in this section, try to visualize your answers. Try to picture whatever it is that comes to mind. You may think of a particular color; if so, that will be your answer. You may think of an element of nature or perhaps a scene from your past. Whatever your answer, make sure it is uniquely your own, whatever feels right to you.

1. I understand that peace can only be found inside myself. No one else can give me peace.

    ☐ Yes

    ☐ No

Peace feels like:

2. I understand that love is a state of mind, and that it exists within me. I am a wellspring of love.

    ☐ Yes

    ☐ No

As it bubbles within me, and out of me, this loving energy feels like:

3. I know I cannot truly love anyone else, not even my own child, unless I truly love myself. I must first experience this feeling within myself, recognize it for what it is, before I can share it.

☐ Yes

☐ No

This sharing of love feels like:

4. On the following pages (or on paper of your own if you prefer), draw pictures for exercises 1-3. (This is not an art contest!)

Peace looks like:

Loving energy looks like:

Sharing love looks like:

5. When my marriage ended, the feelings I had about myself were (draw your feelings):

6. When my marriage ended, my feelings about my spouse were (draw your feelings):

7. Today, as I try to become more nonjudgmental, my feelings for my former spouse are (draw your feelings):

8. Today, as I strive for peace, fulfillment and healing, I see myself as (draw your feelings):

9. As I look toward the future, I want to see my former spouse in that space and time as (draw your feelings):

10. As I look toward the future, I want to see myself in that space and time as (draw your feelings):

Notes and Reflections

Notes and Reflections

Love is a State of Being: our relationship with the Universe.
It is not solely our relationship with another individual.

— Elaine Newell

Chapter 8

Dating, Mating, Relating

For some, this chapter title has a pleasant ring to it. For others, the words and emotional impact behind them promote uneasiness or even fear. Whatever your reaction, this step, along with the steps outlined in chapter two, is a requirement for reaching your goal of a brighter tomorrow, of becoming the woman you have chosen to be. Being a total, well-rounded woman includes being comfortable relating to people—men included. Being a single woman means dating and, quite probably, becoming sexually active again. This is not true for everyone, but it is for a large majority of divorced women.

The logical progression of your development requires that your foundation of inner security be established before embarking upon this step. Don't take it until you are totally, one hundred percent sure you are ready. On the other hand, postponing reentry into the dating scene for too long isn't a good idea either. I know a woman in her late thirties who became such a recluse after her fifteen-year marriage ended that her friends referred to her as "Mother Superior." On the other extreme I know women who can't bear to think of a weekend alone and make the bar scene every Friday and Saturday night, hoping to find "someone to love." There is a happy medium.

Reentering the dating world can be frightening to those who consider themselves middle-aged or beyond. "I wouldn't know how to act on a date. It's been such a long time I'd feel silly!" That may be true in the beginning, but that feeling quickly dispels, and the experience of dating can do wonders for the ego. Rebuilding this part of our human structure is necessary. Now that we are on the path of growth we know that ego has its place, and its place is not at the head of the table; that's where spirit belongs. But we also know that ignoring ego's existence isn't healthy either. It is important to reaffirm that you are still a desirable woman, that a man enjoys spending time with you, spending money on you, maybe spending the night with you. What is of equal importance is that you learn to enjoy the same things in a man.

Your first goal when you begin dating again is to get comfortable being in the presence of men. Not that you've been shut away in an ivory tower, but a single woman is perceived differently by the male populace than a married woman is. (And you will begin to look at men through different eyes, too!) You need to relearn how to relate and communicate with the opposite sex, how to accept men—instead of just one man—into your private world. I also suggest that you begin this step in as casual a manner as possible, and keep your expectations reasonable. It is not necessary to begin looking right away for *la grande passion.*

Well, okay, if that's what's required, then how do we go about it? After all, the man shortage is not a well-kept secret.

There are a number of ways.

Letting family and friends know you are ready to begin dating is one. Someone in your circle probably knows an eligible bachelor. They can arrange a quiet dinner party where the intent is not all that obvious. Cocktail parties or, if the season is right, office parties where guests are invited are other subtle settings. Of course, since you've become a member of a couple of organizations, you have the opportunity of meeting people on your own, too.

Singles dances and singles organizations are also a good bet. Organizations offer planned activities such as game nights, dine arounds, sports activities. Anything wherein a group gets together on a regular basis is a more relaxed way of getting acquainted. Many churches have singles groups.

A few of the women I interviewed told me they had met people through answering ads in the personal columns of newspapers and magazines. I have a personal bias against this method. It is not only dangerous—whatever "screening" takes place is what you do solely on the telephone—but the success rate of these encounters is minimal.

A good percentage of women told me they found the safest way to get back into circulation is to use dating services. These agencies come in a variety of wrappings, although most are fairly costly. The advantage they offer is assuring you that the men you will meet are single—a prerequisite to a healthy relationship—and matching you with someone with whom you have something in common.

Keeping an optimistic attitude will help you get past some of the hurdles. The old saying, "You have to kiss a lot of frogs before you find a prince," is not far from the truth. But since you are not looking for a deep and meaningful relationship—at least not right away—you should not be too disappointed. Above all else it is necessary to remember who you are and what you want and do not want in a relationship, and stick to your guns! Keep an open mind, and a ready sense of humor will see you through.

Let's take a peek now at some of the experiences of our sisters, remembering that your own path will probably follow similar turns.

Melissa, a forty-year-old woman with a striking figure and twinkling gray eyes, kept a journal during the first year or so following her divorce: reviewing it offered several good belly laughs, which she shares here.

"One fella I'll never forget was 'Eddie, the Egg Man. I met Eddie through a dating service. We met for our date in the parking lot of a local restaurant, except Eddie didn't like that particular spot and suggested another. So we drove, in separate cars, to this place that turned out to be nothing more than a diner. 'Well okay,' I said to myself, 'after all, this is a blind date, so I can't really blame him for wanting to keep expenses down.'

105

"Eddie was an okay-looking guy, maybe even a little above average. Well, while we looked over the menu Eddie let me in on his dietary secrets. He looked at me with this kind of sly smile and he said, 'I'm very careful about what I eat. Actually the only things I eat are steak, hamburger, potatoes, and peas if they don't wrinkle.'

"You can imagine my reaction to that one! Somehow I managed to keep my cool and not look too surprised. I guess I said something like, 'If they don't wrinkle?'

"'Yeah,' he said, 'you know how sometimes when you cook frozen peas they get kind of all wrinkly?'

"I tried to look as if I knew what he was talking about, which of course I didn't. Then he leaned across the table and whispered, 'I'm fifty-six years old and I've never eaten an egg.'

"I know my mouth flew open at that one. I finally asked him, 'Why not?' and he said, 'Haven't you noticed how they smell?'

"By this time I'm thinking I've got a nut on my hands. Harmless, but really a little squirrely. Then he said, 'It's not just how they smell, it's where they come from.'

"That did it. I figured I'd wasted enough time. I looked him square in the eye and said, 'And just where do you think you came from, buddy?' I left Eddie sitting there in that dingy diner poking his fork at his wrinkly peas. Thank heaven I'd had the good sense to bring my own car."

Chuckling softly, Melissa continued reminiscing. "The next one was Charles. Now Charles had possibilities! He was handsome, educated, well spoken. We shared common interests in food, which was a plus after Eddie, and the great thing was, he seemed totally smitten by me. Again, it was a blind date. This time we met over cocktails. About halfway through the second drink, Charles leaned across the table and said in this really husky kind of voice, 'You are the most intriguing woman I've met in five years. When can I see you again?'

"Well, I was trying to keep things in perspective, and you know, sort of play it cool, but I guess I did manage to say something like, 'I believe I'm free this weekend.'

"Then Charles began talking about all the places he wanted to take me, and things he wanted us to do together, the people he wanted me to meet. Then when we left the lounge he walked me to my car and kind of brushed my cheek with his lips, and he said, 'I don't know how I'll manage to wait until the weekend.' I can tell you I floated home.

"Well, the weekend came and went and so did the next one. And so did Charles. I never heard from him again. But he had served a purpose. Charles helped me without knowing it. It was the first time I'd felt desirable in a long time and I realized how good it felt. It didn't really matter that Charles was a bit of a cad with a line as long as his arm. He triggered something in me I'd almost forgotten. I really am a desirable and interesting woman, and I don't need anyone else to tell me that. I know it within myself. Charles served the purpose of reminding me, and I make it a point not to forget again."

Many of the women I interviewed had similar stories to tell with only minor changes in character and dialogue. Some of these encounters were quite humorous. Some were plain boring. A few were wrestling matches. But the important thing was, these women were learning to relate to men again. They were finding out things about themselves—what they really liked and didn't like—and they were repairing their battered egos. For most, an emotional involvement did occur in time, but not before they'd had some practice, and not before they had again learned the give and take of male-female relationships.

For those women who were willing to wait until they were ready for an emotional involvement, the story was much the same. They were healed enough to enter into a new relationship, freed from the past. For those who didn't wait, who didn't do the foundation work, it was a different story.

Bea is a beautiful young woman in her mid-forties—blonde, articulate, keeps herself in good shape, and has a creative flair that manifests itself in her home, garden, and dress. She was thirty-eight when her husband left her for another woman, whom he later married. Bea had fought with everything in her to preserve her marriage, even after it became apparent that she was the only one interested in the preservation. Her husband was and had always been a compulsive womanizer, a fact Bea had denied on the conscious level throughout the fifteen-year marriage. When she finally found the courage to face the truth, and a divorce, she was left with two young sons to raise and limited work experience. The love she had once felt for her husband turned to a deep, consuming hatred. She fought for and won the home, the furnishings, the boat, both cars, custody of the children, and substantial child support. When he asked for the golfing trophies he'd won, her answer was a flat "No."

Within six weeks following the separation from her husband, Bea entered into her first affair. It was short-lived but quickly followed by another of similar duration. At the end of six months she met Jim, an alcoholic. This affair lasted off and on for two years. During this period Bea tried, without success, to turn Jim into the man she had imagined her husband to be: caring, expressive of his feelings, a romantic lover. Her new partner was poorly equipped to fulfill such a role. When the affair ended Bea was left with an even deeper wound to her ego, and an even greater desire to find the man of her dreams. The fact that she wasn't dealing with her unresolved rage, rage at her ex-mate and at Jim, was only a vague and passing thought. The fact that she was looking to others for fulfillment had not yet entered her consciousness.

Although Bea's role as a single parent was time and energy consuming, she still found time to continue her search for the perfect partner. It was a mere two months after Jim's departure that she met Peter.

Peter was a recovering alcoholic. He'd been sober three years at the time Bea met him; however, his attendance at AA meetings had waned and he suffered from periodic bouts of depression. In essence, Peter was on a "dry drunk." The alcoholic behavior patterns Bea had seen in Jim were reflected in Peter, and the roving eye tendencies of Bea's former husband were also a part of Peter's makeup. The relationship lasted for approximately three years, during which time they split up and reunited numerous times. The resumption of the affair was always Bea's doing. In essence, she was repeating all the behavior patterns of the past—

fighting to hold onto a relationship that was damaging her emotionally.

The pattern continued for some time. Bea's divorce certificate was eight years old before she entered therapy and took her first positive steps toward personal growth and emotional freedom. Today, in her own words, "I finally got it together—but it sure took a while!"

Bea's story is not uncommon, and it is typical of women who search outside themselves for happiness and fulfillment. Expecting our personal happiness to come from or through another person is unrealistic. It's also impossible. Our happiness springs from our own inner well. It is only after we have tapped this well and drunk from it deeply that we are ready and capable of sharing our joy with others. Once we do find it, we will look for partners who drink from their own spring. Like does attract like. If you have any doubt, take a good, deep look at your closest friends. Invariably, they mirror some aspect of yourself, which is why they are in your life—so you can learn from them.

One phenomenon among divorced women occurs with such regularity I would be remiss in not mentioning it here. It can occur at any time, but unfortunately it often happens during the early and most painful period following divorce. I call it "The Best Friend Syndrome."

It usually comes in the guise of your ex's best friend, although it can be your best girlfriend's husband or even your next-door neighbor. Over ninety percent of the women I've talked with have experienced it, and it goes something like this.

You need somebody to help you out of a jam. You have a problem with your washing machine or automobile or any number of situations in which you feel the need to call upon a male friend.

"Best Friend" arrives to save "Damsel in Distress." Oh, he probably fixes the washing machine all right, but then for reasons known only to the male psyche, he assumes your internal plumbing is in need of "flushing out" too, and he makes a pass. If you have viewed this man only as a friend, or perhaps as your best friend's husband, this can be quite upsetting. Make no mistake about the "affection" being offered; you are being perceived as an easy target!

You are a woman undergoing major crises, and this "opportunist" moves in to take advantage of the situation. There is only one way to handle it. Face it head on and stand your ground! Sometimes a steely-eyed glare will do it; for the more insensitive types a cryptic remark is required. If the man is particularly aggressive it may mean a real confrontation. Whatever it takes, do it!

Make no mistake, this is not flattery. This is insult. This man has broken your trust, and taking him up on his "original idea" is just about as counterproductive to regaining your emotional health as anything can be. If you really need sex, look elsewhere. The family "Best Friend" is not on the agenda. The grace with which you handle the situation will determine your future relationship with this man and with his wife. You've also learned something about the state of your "Best Friend's" marriage.

Surprises of this nature will be part of your new life. You will undoubtedly learn things you would rather not know, but the wiser we are, the better equipped we are to face life and all its many (more often than not, wondrous) facets.

Being human means being sexual. Sexuality is as much a part of our nature as is our spirituality. As a matter of fact our spiritual energy and our sexual energy are similar. Spirit manifests through thought and action; the same is true of sexuality. When we marry, we choose our partner for a variety of reasons, one of which is sexual. We want to be with someone we are physically attracted to. We want to express our sexuality with and through this person. When the marriage ends, these feelings do not just go away. When you reenter the mainstream of life again by dating and associating with men, the subject of sex will quite naturally surface. And if it does happen that way—naturally—it is by far the best way. Contrived sexual encounters tend to be left wanting in the tenderness department. What you do about sex is, of course, an individual choice. The important thing is to make sure that whatever occurs is indeed your choice.

Your first sexual encounter (first since the divorce, that is) can be something you look forward to with anticipation or trepidation, depending on your attitude and basic nature. If the timing is such that it occurs when you are truly ready for it, it can be an experience you will cherish in the years ahead.

Following is my own story of this event, and I share it with you in the hope it will alleviate some of your apprehension. I consider myself fortunate that this experience happened in the particular way it did.

I met Frank through one of the organizations I'd joined and came to know him on a social and intellectual level before our friendship deepened. Since we were both single it seemed quite natural to occasionally call each other and suggest events to visit together. One such occasion was a weekend trip to a New England island, where Frank's buddy's boat was moored. He had extended Frank an invitation to spend the weekend, suggesting he bring along a friend. The trip over to the island by ferry was invigorating. I have always found sea air to be a balm to my senses, and even before we were underway, I found myself relaxing for the first time in a long, long time. The tensions I'd been carrying in the year since my divorce seemed to be slipping away.

The island was quaint, the friend's boat roomy and comfortable, but the motor was acting up. So instead of going for a sail, Frank and I spent the morning walking the country roads and poking through the tiny shops. Then we returned to the boat for lunch and a rest. While Frank and his friend tinkered around with the motor below, I took a book and stretched out on deck. After a few minutes I laid the book aside and gazed out at the harbor.

Off to the left, just rounding the stern of a neighboring boat, a majestic white swan sailed into view. He paused, turned his head to look at me, then changed direction and headed toward me. I watched the exquisite creature, intrigued at how well he seemed to tolerate the civilization around him: sails ruffling, laughter from the boat parties, masts clinking in the breeze. He looked proud, yet somehow a little sad. I coaxed him over to the boat and offered him the remains of my sandwich. Just then, Frank stuck his head up through the hatch, and I gestured toward our visitor.

111

"Oh, yes, he's been around for quite a while," Frank said. "Evidently he's lost his mate, because there were always two of them before, but for the last several weeks he's been going it alone. Swans mate for life, you know."

I thought my heart would break. I looked back at the swan with new understanding. His partner was gone, but alone and obviously aching, he still held his head high and he was going about his business as usual, doing the best he could in spite of his pain. The tears welled up and spilled over, and when Frank saw them, he gave me a thumbs up and again disappeared below deck.

I sat for a long time watching the swan as he made his rounds through the harbor. Periodically, he would turn and look back at me—as if he knew and understood. It was a rare and poignant moment of communication.

Somewhere around mid-afternoon Frank's friend received an emergency phone call from the mainland and had to return home. He left Frank in charge of the boat with instructions on how to close it up when we would leave next day.

Frank and I went to a nice little spot for dinner and later stopped by a couple of clubs for dancing and drinks. It was after midnight as we made our way back through the narrow, twisting streets. When we reached the beach we took off our shoes and walked barefoot in the wet sand. It wasn't long before we were holding hands. The night sky was beautiful beyond description, the rolling surf teasing at our feet.

We paddled the dinghy out to the boat and climbed aboard. Frank immediately went below while I chose to sit a while on deck still enjoying the tranquility of the night. When Frank reappeared a few moments later and sat next to me, I said something like, "I guess it's time for you to show me where I sleep."

He looked at me intently for a moment, then with a little half smile he said, "We're going to sleep in the captain's quarters, aren't we?"

I can't say it was a surprise, but the way he said it was. Obviously, he could read my confusion. I didn't know what to say, so I said nothing. Gently, he took my hand between his own.

112

"We're both adults, we care for each other, and I think we should sleep in the captain's quarters. What do you think?"

The ball was in my park. There was no pressure. The decision was entirely mine. Whichever way I chose I knew it would be all right for Frank. It was my moment of truth. I didn't try to analyze it. I didn't intellectualize it. I went with my intuition. "You've had some pretty good ideas today," I said finally, "but this is one of the best. Yes, I think we should sleep in the captain's quarters tonight."

And we did. And it was incredibly tender and caring and altogether beautiful. I didn't think even one time about my former marriage partner. This was new and truly comfortable and not in the least threatening or fearful. Frank was the ideal initiator. There was no pretending about "being in love," no words of love were spoken. There was a mutual need of two people who really liked each other.

I saw Frank at meetings and social gatherings for several months after that before he took a job out-of-state and moved away. Although we felt a deep devotion to one another, there was never another sexual encounter, or even an indication of one. And that was okay. In fact it was perfect. Our one night together was precisely that. We both knew this was not a love affair. For a few brief hours we had enjoyed coming together, being together, and it was indeed, a night to remember.

Exercises

Love is a state of mind and a state of being. True love begins with loving ourselves and expands outward as far as we are willing to let it go. More than our relationship to a particular person, it is our relationship to the world.

1. I realize that in order to become a fully functional single woman, I must include single men in my roster of friends.

    ☐ Yes

    ☐ No

    ☐ Maybe

2. When I consider dating again, I feel:

    ☐ Uncomfortable

    ☐ Frightened by the thought of sex

    ☐ Hopeful

    ☐ Eager

    ☐ Out of sync

    ☐ Frigid

    ☐ Desirable

    ☐ Lost

    ☐ Confident

    ☐ Intimidated

    ☐ Ready to go

    ☐ Enthusiastic

    ☐ Unprepared

    ☐ Other (Explain:)

3. Now think about your "Woman of Tomorrow." Looking at your checklist above, are there areas you need to work on in order to reach your goal?

☐ Yes

☐ No

☐ Some

4. If there are areas/points you need to work on in order to obtain your goal, explain what you plan to do:

5. When I look toward the future I can see myself:

☐ Married

☐ Single

6. In the future I would like to be:

☐ Married

☐ Single

7. Explain the reasons for your answers to #5 and #6:

8. I am comfortable in relating to men I work with:

☐ Yes

☐ No

9. I am comfortable with men who are married or otherwise unavailable:

☐ Yes

☐ No

10. I am comfortable with available men:

☐ Yes

☐ No

Notes and Reflections

Notes and Reflections

Forgiveness is letting what was, be gone;
What will be, come; What is now, be.

— David Augsburger

Chapter 9

Leaving with Love

I remember reading a long time ago about a famous writer (it might have been Hemingway) who, when questioned by an interviewer as to why in the early days of his career he had persevered in spite of all the rejection, answered, "I found it less painful to write than not to write."

Not long ago I heard a woman say something similar on the subject of forgiveness. When asked why or how she could honestly say she had forgiven her husband (he had plotted to have her killed in order to get her money), she explained, "I found, after a lot of agonizing, that it was simply too painful not to forgive him."

Buddha spoke often on the subject of forgiveness. He said: True forgiveness is an act of the highest of human behavior.

Those who have practiced forgiveness in their own lives attest that it is also the closest thing to true freedom the human mind can experience.

Mountains of material have been written on the subject of forgiveness—enough words spoken to envelop the planet a thousand times—but why is forgiveness so important? Why is it so vital to our mental and emotional well-being to forgive the offense—no matter how heinous? Once

119

we've gotten over the shock, why can't we just go our merry way (hoping that someday the offender will "get his") and be done with it? When someone wrongs us, causes us pain, behaves in a manner which we do not understand or accept, our view of that person changes. We see something we did not see before. Sometimes we are so distressed by the other person's behavior that we forget all the good things in that person, all the things we loved about him, all the years of a "good" relationship. It is only when we pause to remember that we too are human—that we too are capable of causing someone pain, that under a given set of circumstances we too could shatter another person's belief in us—can we begin to realize and acknowledge that we are neither saints or sinners but fellow travelers. As human beings we share the same human traits. We are all capable of feats of courage and compassion, deception and ruthlessness. But which traits we continue to develop as adults are of our own choosing.

At our soul level, what we see out there in the world is but a mirror image of what we are inside. On this wondrous stage we call life, we are offered the opportunity to play many roles—hero/villain, victim/perpetrator, jailer/prisoner, dependent/protector—and the subtlety with which these roles change is part of the adventure.

No matter what part we are currently playing, we will at some point in time be given the opportunity to play the opposite role. This is one of the universal laws. This is part of the "testing" of life. This is where we are offered opportunities for growth. This is where lessons can be learned.

In Act I, we may be the innocent victim of abuse, but by Act III the plot has twisted until we are now in a position to rain the same terror on our persecutor. Will we accept the role or decline? Will we seek revenge or offer compassion?

Of all the numerous studies made about human beings under stress, few are more interesting than those regarding the experience of death. Primary among the researchers in this field is Dr. Elisabeth Kübler-Ross, a woman whose life's work has been dedicated to helping the dying make a peaceful transition from the earth plane through God's Other Door. There are numerous documented accounts of people who have begun this experience and then, for whatever reason, returned to tell about it. While these reports fill many volumes, there is one underlying theme.

These people tell of passing through a long, dark tunnel. At the far end of this tunnel, a beautiful, compelling light beckoned to them. They were drawn to this light by the sheer love that radiates from it. As these people moved nearer to the light, they were overwhelmed by a sense of peace and well-being. They walked toward the light with eager anticipation.

The interesting point is that not everyone who walked this tunnel experienced it in the same way. Many people spoke of seeing deceased loved ones who greeted them, reached out to embrace them as they made their way toward the light. These loving encounters only increased the individual's feelings of joy and contentment. Others, however, spoke of creatures of the dark grasping at them from the shadows of the tunnel, tearing at their clothing, clutching at them and trying to draw them away from the light. They said they knew there was safety in the light and wanted very much to go to it, but these "other beings" were trying to stop them from getting there.

Why would this experience be joyful for some and terrifying for others? Could it be that those who had a negative death experience were afraid to die? Fear was present in some cases, but certainly not in all. Many of those who had a peaceful "passing" were also afraid and extremely reluctant to let go of what we call "life."

I have talked with many people who have had this experience, and in these conversations one fact always surfaced rather quickly: Those who experienced peace had expected peace. These were peaceful people who projected positive attitudes. They generated love and they received it in return.

Those who spoke of the experience as being fearful were people of a much less positive outlook. They were suspicious of just about everything, including the medical care they received at the time of their experience. They spoke of the wrongs that had been done to them throughout their lives. In short, they expected to be treated badly;

they expected every encounter to be difficult, and that is what they experienced.

This leads us to contemplate whether we do indeed get back what we send out. Every self-help book we browse and every church we pass counsel us: "To have love, give love," "If you want a friend, be a friend," and "Do unto others as you would have others do unto you." The further we go down life's pathway, the more apparent it becomes that giving and receiving (like love and hate) are one and the same. As one young woman puts it, "It's all a giant carousel. Everything is a circle." Or to use the vernacular, "What goes around comes around."

Perhaps then, when we speak of this thing "forgiveness," acceptance may be the key—acceptance of our own humanity as well as the humanity of others. Accept the truth that yes, others can betray us, as we can betray ourselves. Haven't we all at some time let ourselves down? Haven't we told a lie that we later regretted? Haven't we wronged a loved one, knowing full well what we were doing at the time?

Jesus, speaking to the throng who gathered to stone the adulteress, said, "He that is without sin among you, let him first cast a stone at her" (John 8:7). And in the sermon on the mount, he said, "Ye are the light of the world" (Matthew 5:14). He was reminding us of our humanity as well as our spirituality.

To believe in the continuum of life is to believe in the continuum of love, since true love springs from spirit and spirit is eternal. Once love happens, it is forever. In marriage we come together to honor the love we feel for each other. As time goes by, that love changes, grows, takes on different hues, or stagnates and pales. Occasionally, when one of us is attracted to a new lover, a new way of life, a new whatever, we tell ourself the love we felt before has died. This is an easy way out because the human psyche can accept death. What we have difficulty accepting is that love changes.

In spirit, we join in order to learn from one another, to see in the other what is real within ourselves. As long as the relationship serves to aid our spiritual growth, it will continue. Once the lesson has been learned, the relationship begins to change. That isn't to say there aren't other lessons we can learn from our partner; most probably there are, but in this vast eternity of spiritual experience it is reasonable to assume there are others from whom we can learn other lessons, too. And so we move on. Perhaps a large part of our need for change is that we have shown our vulnerability to our mate, and we are ashamed. We fear that he has seen us for what we truly are; some of us concentrate so fully on the negatives, forgetting the positives we have shown, that the need to start afresh becomes necessary to us. We forget, or deny, our oneness with our brothers, seeing ourselves as separated and apart from those who know us best. This is what really happens when long-term marriages end. Oh, we find a myriad reasons—he got fat, he had an affair, he's an alcoholic, he's become cold and neglectful—we are very good at making up our own script; but the spiritual reason for the "break up" is simply that we have learned what we came together to learn and have chosen to move on.

Sometimes both parties reach the same realization at more or less the same time; often they do not. One will want to continue the union on the same terms as before, fearful of accepting the changes taking place, while the other partner "knows" it is time to change the game—and maybe the players. This is the pain of divorce—the rejection to the ego. If we could look at it from the level of spirit, we would see that love has not died, did not end, and is eternal. It has merely changed.

Some of us can remember the physical pain of growing up, when the bones in our legs hurt. When we complained to an adult, we received a pat on the head accompanied with the explanation, "Oh, it's only growing pains. It will pass." And pass it did. Nevertheless, it was painful. But we were locked into the situation; there was nothing we could do. Our body was growing, and we had no say in the matter. Let's suppose for a minute we did have a choice. Let's suppose that one long, dark night when the pain was intense, we just decided, "All right, I'll just stop growing!" Maybe we were five or six years old at the time; certainly not very big. Imagine how difficult it would be to function in our world of today, trapped in the body of a six year old.

The same principle applies of course, to spiritual growth. We can choose to stop growing. We can determine that we are not going to learn the lessons before us. We can live our lives stunted emotionally and spiritually. But is this what we truly want? There is another way, and that is to acknowledge the pain, release it, and let it go.

As long as we hold onto the pain of unforgiveness, we place a tremendous block on our path to emotional freedom. As long as we deny our higher potential, we stunt our own growth. Forgiveness, then, is not so much for the other guy as it is for ourself. True, the other person will benefit from our removal of the negative energy with which we have bombarded him, but the soul that does the forgiving reaps the greater benefit because the blockage to its own growth has been removed. As we draw nearer to our recognition and acceptance of "the oneness," the more eager we become to forgive, for in forgiving another we forgive ourself. In forgiving another we forgive all. In forgiving we accept our oneness as humans, and our Oneness in Spirit.

Exercises

Unforgiveness is the baggage we carry strapped to our minds that makes our bones brittle and our hearts bitter. If your Woman of Tomorrow is a happy, contented, functional, self-fulfilled woman, at peace with herself, then you'll have to drop any remnants of unrelenting unforgiveness.

The greatest lesson any of us has to learn is forgiveness—of self as well as of others. It is the advanced curriculum of human experience, and we all take the course. Whatever hardship you are facing now, recognize it as an opportunity to grow. If you choose not to learn the lesson of forgiveness from this current experience, rest assured you will be offered another opportunity. The choice is yours.

"Forgive us our trespasses as we forgive those who trespass against us." In other words, we have a share in this. There is a payoff. It's our spirit that grows through forgiveness.

1. I am willing to accept that I am in the right place at the right time and that universal law is governing my life.

   ☐ Yes

   ☐ No

   ☐ Unsure

2. I am willing to accept my own role in my current circumstances, knowing the events which brought me to this time and place were Divinely inspired in order to bring me to the point of self-realization.

   ☐ Yes

   ☐ No

   ☐ Unsure

3. I trust in the rightful outcome of my affairs, believing that everything works for the good no matter how upsetting it may appear at the moment.

   ☐ Yes

   ☐ No

   ☐ Unsure

4. I acknowledge there are no stepchildren in the universe, and that my Creator loves all His/Her children (my former spouse included) as much as He/She loves me.

☐ Yes

☐ No

☐ Unsure

5. I believe that the force which governs the universe is love and not fear.

☐ Yes

☐ No

☐ Unsure

6. I realize that the release of emotional pain takes place within my own mind.

☐ Yes

☐ No

☐ Unsure

7. I understand this process to be: Address it, bless it, let it go.

☐ Yes

☐ No

☐ Unsure

Notes and Reflections

Notes and Reflections

Identify with love and you are safe. Identify with love and you are home. Identify with love, and find your Self.
— *A Course in Miracles*

Chapter 10

The New You

Accepting where we are now, as opposed to where we were, takes some good, hard looking. Sometimes it's hard to see the change in ourself. The things we've left behind, the people we've left behind, are to be accepted for their unique and wondrous place in our life. We can bless and thank each person who has crossed our path, because if they had not walked across our landscape, we would not be who we are. We would be different because we would have missed the wonderful opportunities for learning that these precious souls brought into our life. And now, if they are gone from our view, let us tuck them away in their own tiny corner of our heart and never, never for one moment forget to be thankful for their gifts to us.

Let us also remember that because of our presence in their lives, they too have been given the opportunity for spiritual growth. We have played our role in their play, changed their lives with our energy, our own unique being.

And now we have come to the end of one dramatic play in our lives. The lights have gone down; the curtain descended. For a while, we are left in a darkened theater, unsure of where to turn next. Should we look for the exit and run away? Or sit for a while in the darkness, allowing our eyes to become accustomed to the unfamiliar shapes around us? Maybe we run into the ladies' room for a brief period and cry our eyes out because the play is over, but when we return to the theater, although it is still dark, we take a different seat, this time in the balcony from where we can get an overview.

Now, gradually, the house lights come back, the orchestra files in and takes its place in the orchestra pit. The players are waiting in the wings for their cue. We realize a wonderful new "opening night" is about to take place. The overture begins. The music is new. Part of our new production. Our play. Our music. We wrote the script, designed the sets, created the musical score and lyrics.

What will this new play be about? What kind of woman will the heroine be? Is this a romantic love story? Is it the story of a career woman who struggles her way to the top? Perhaps it is about a gentle and peaceful woman who becomes a wise counsel to those who share her life?

As with every playwright, we will be surprised at some of the "intricacies" of our own play. One character reads a line a little differently than we had intended, and it works well! The audience is laughing, happy that the leading man turned the phrase in just that way! Isn't it wonderful that our own script can offer some breathtaking surprises? Why, it's a whole new adventure—a wonderful new way to look at life. With everything that is happening in this new production, it's a little hard to look back at that other play, because we're so excited about experiencing this new one.

Oh, there will be moments when we will look back and say, "No, I didn't like the ending of that other play. I had expected it to be more of a romantic comedy than the melodrama it turned out to be. But, on the other hand, it did have its good moments. Even some great ones." And then we reclaim our place and continue experiencing the new production, gradually allowing the earlier play to take its rightful place in the past. It truly is so much nicer this way, letting the present be our main interest and not allowing the past to overshadow what is currently on stage.

Clair B. Ludlow, in her little book *A Bridge to Peace,* writes,

While many of us want to choose to experience love we find it challenging to give up old habits of responding defensively to the world. Our fears and guilts from the past block our ability to extend and receive love in the present. We can let go of the past by acknowledging and forgiving our fears in the light of our true identity of love.

So we continue our play, each day creating new scenes that will appear on our stage of tomorrow, filling each day with whatever joys we care to show forth in our new story. We are, after all, totally responsible for this production.

Exercises

Any crisis we face in life changes us. Challenges are the means by which we grow or regress. Ultimately, we determine the outcome. When the time of testing has passed, only then are we capable of evaluating the direction we took, forward or backward.

Perhaps you are still in the thick of your crisis. Perhaps you are not in a place, as yet, to evaluate where you have come from and in which direction you are moving. If that is the case, please save this last exercise for a later time. However, if you have begun your path through healing, please take as much time and space as you need to evaluate your own path through the woods. Try to be as objective as you can.

May your heart and mind be ever open
To the joyous release of forgiveness
And may your spirit be forever tuned
To the peace and love of your Creator.

Notes and Reflections

Notes and Reflections

Works Cited and Recommended

Works Cited

Biblical references throughout are taken from the Authorized King James Version.

Chapter 1

Butterworth, Eric. *Spiritual Economics: The Prosperity Process*. Unity Village, Missouri: Unity School of Christianity, 1983. Page 21.

Chapter 2

Peck, M. Scott. *The Road Less Traveled*. New York: Touchstone, 1978. Page 266.

Chapter 3

Congreve, William. *The Mourning Bride*. Act III, scene 8. As cited in *Bartlett's Familiar Quotations*. Boston: Little Brown & Company, 1955. Page 254.

Chapter 5

Gawain, Shakti. *Reflections in the Light*. San Rafael, California: New World Library, 1988. Page 49.

Chapter 6

Hotchkiss, Burt. *Have Miracles Will Travel*. Sweet Home, Oregon: Fernwood Management, 1982. Page 14.

Chapter 7

Gilbert, Arthur. *The Passover Seder: Pathways Through the Haggadah*. Hoboken, New Jersey: Klav Publishing, Inc., 1970.

Chapter 9

Augsburger, David. As quoted in Buscaglia, Leo. *Loving Each Other: The Challenge of Human Relationships*. Thorofare, New Jersey: Slack Inc., 1984. Page 101.

Chapter 10

A Course in Miracles. Tiburon, California: Foundation for Inner Peace, 1975. Workbook for Students, page 415.

Ludlow, Claire B. *Bridge to Peace*. Amherst, Massachusetts: Harmonie Institute, Inc., 1987. Page 3.

Recommended Reading

Bradshaw, John. *Creating Love: The Next Great Stage of Growth*. New York: Bantam Books, 1992.

Buscaglia, Leo. *Loving Each Other: The Challenge of Human Relationships*. Thorofare, New Jersey: Slack Inc., 1984.

A Course in Miracles. Tiburon, California: Foundation for Inner Peace, 1975.

Eadie, Betty J. *Embraced by the Light*. Placerville, California: Gold Leaf Press, 1992.

Hay, Louise L. *You Can Heal Your Life*. Carson, California: Hay House, 1993.

Hotchkiss, Burt. *Your Owner's Manual*. Sweet Home, Oregon: Fernwood Management, 1993.

Jampolsky, Gerald G. *Love Is Letting Go of Fear*. Berkeley: Celestial Arts, 1979.

Ryan, Barbara Shlemon. *Healing the Wounds of Divorce*. Notre Dame, Indiana: Ave Maria Press, 1990.

Williamson, Marianne. *A Return to Love*. New York: HarperCollins, 1992.

———. *A Woman's Worth*. New York: Random House, 1993.